Hidden Treasure

Hidden Treasure
Digging up Britain's Past

Dr Neil Faulkner

Foreword by
Miranda Krestovnikoff

BOOKS

To the conscientious metal-detectorist, who removes finds only from disturbed ground, records find-spots, and reports regularly to the local archaeological authorities.

The conscientious metal-detectorist is a salvage archaeologist rescuing our heritage.

This book is published to accompany the television series *Hidden Treasure*, which was first broadcast on BBC Television in 2003.

Executive producer: John Farren
Series producer: Ian Potts
Directors: Clare Duncan, Dan Kendal, Melisa Osman, Marc Ramsay
Researchers: Monika Kupper, Kate Murray, William Spiers
Production co-ordinators: Xanthe Apostolos, Helen Partridge, Hayley Vermeulen
Production manager: Alison Woolnough
Production executive: Anna Mishcon

First published in 2003
Copyright © Neil Faulkner 2003
The moral right of the author has been asserted.

ISBN 0 563 48790 9

Published by BBC Books, BBC Worldwide Ltd,
Woodlands, 80 Wood Lane, London W12 0TT

Commissioning editor: Sally Potter
Project editor: Warren Albers
Art director: Linda Blakemore
Designer: DW Design, London
Picture research: Charlotte Lochhead
Production controller: Belinda Rapley

Set in Berling and Quay
Printed and bound in Great Britain by Butler and Tanner Ltd, Frome
Colour separations by Radstock Reproductions Ltd, Midsomer Norton
Jacket printed by Lawrence-Allen Ltd, Western-super-Mare

CONTENTS

Foreword

As a zoologist, I tend to march around the countryside looking all around me – up at the trees searching for the birds and other wildlife that have fascinated me since my childhood. Filming *Hidden Treasure* changed all that. I still hear the birds and smell the flowers but my thoughts are elsewhere. I now stroll more slowly, with my head down, scouring the ground beneath my feet for clues of what might lie hidden there. Fieldwalkers all over the country do just this and, combined with metal-detecting, this has led to the remarkable finds featured in the television series and this book.

I'd never even *held* a metal-detector until we started filming, and on only my second attempt I found a silver Iron Age coin. The last person to touch that coin lived over 2,000 years ago. Just imagine that … how spoilt I've been! I now always expect to find exciting artefacts on dig sites because I've had the privilege of detecting and digging on some of the most interesting and productive sites recently discovered in the UK. I've also been allowed to handle rare and magnificent objects from museums, which most people can only hope to peer at in a secured glass cabinet. The whole experience has been unforgettable.

As a child I used to be fascinated with the old glass bottles that would come up from time to time when digging our vegetable patch – I never believed that it would lead to a job in presenting archaeology. What a steep learning curve it's been, too. To be an archaeologist you need a good imagination – something I'm learning to develop. You have to stand in the middle of a trench in the middle of a field (invariably in the cold and wet) gazing at a few bits of broken bone, flint and pot and imagine what people were doing there hundreds, even thousands, of years ago. It's tough, but gradually, when the experts put these items in their context – how they were used in ritual sacrifice, feasting and ceremony – you start to get the picture of life in Ancient Britain.

I can't imagine what it is like to find a Roman burial site or a hoard of Iron Age coins – I know that if it were me, my first instinct would be to dig and dig until I'd uncovered the whole hoard. Our finders have managed to put their excitement to one side, and once they realized how significant their finds were, they contacted local archaeologists who were then able to excavate the sites carefully so that the items were kept in their context. You'll hear the word 'context' again and again – it's so important in archaeology. Many artefacts are useless in terms of giving us information unless we know where they came from and what other items they were associated with.

My plea to anyone who watches the series or reads this book is: don't think that if you go out and buy a detector that you will find items like the ones we show in a few days or weeks. Most of our finders have been detecting for many years. They seek permission to search the land they detect on, they show finds and split rewards with the landowner and they act responsibly when finds are made – reporting them to the local finds liaison officer as part of the Portable Antiquities Scheme (more about this in the book and series). It can be a long process and many people never find gold or silver in their lifetime. You need patience, but the hobby will captivate you and draw you into finding out more about local history and archaeology.

During the last six months, I've had the great privilege of working with an unparalleled team of experts, museum curators, archaeologists and enthusiastic metal-detecting groups from around the country. This is not to mention our wonderful group of contributors, who are set apart not only because they *found* these amazing objects, but also because of their immense enthusiasm, knowledge of their subject, and huge sacrifice of time for our filming.

The eight programmes in the series, on which this book is based, took many months to research and then film (mostly, as I remember, in the unfavourable and rather disheartening weather conditions we have in this country) and I would like to thank Ian Potts (the series producer) and all the production team who have held umbrellas, fed me tea and chocolate and generally held the whole thing together. Thanks goodness for thermal underwear and waterproofs!

Miranda Krestovnikoff, June 2003

Lindisfarne

Yeavering

Treasure-site   Key-site

Bronze Age
Iron Age
Roman Britain
Anglo-Saxon

Viking invasion site

Jarrow

Hadrian's Wall

N

W   E

S

Wetwang
East Riding find

D A N E L A W

North Lincolnshire find

Lindow

Llyn Cerrig Bach   Mold

Snettisham

Spong Hill

Leicestershire hoard

West Stow

Sutton Hoo

Ipswich
Anglo-Saxon cemetery

Baldock

Wheathampstead

Camulodunu
(Colchester)

Verulamium (St Albans)

Londinium (London)

Bath

Ringlemere

Avebury

Dover

Stonehenge

Winchester hoard

Fishbourne

Rillaton

60 km

60 miles

Introduction

This book is about digging up the past. This makes it different from most books about archaeology. Usually these present the results of field surveys, excavation and work on finds: they tell us what the experts have discovered about rituals in the Bronze Age, frescoes in Roman villas, or the origins of Anglo-Saxon kingship. They tell us much less about how things get discovered, who makes the discoveries and the great excitement aroused by a discovery that is unexpected and spectacular. Those books that do deal with archaeological methods tend to be rather serious. They often give the impression that the process of discovery is complex and technical, and very much the province of the expert. There is a preoccupation with obscure things like 'contexts' and 'stratigraphy' and 'Harris matrices' that can be off-putting to the newcomer. It is easy to get the impression that archaeology is something for specialists only.

How much, anyway, is there left to find? Have not all the great discoveries already happened? There has been so much archaeology over the last century, and so many great advances in knowledge about the past, that it is difficult to believe there is much left to discover. Certainly, we now have a far better historical framework. We no longer believe that Stonehenge was built by druids, for example, or that every earthwork was 'Caesar's camp'. However, we should not fall into the common error of thinking that knowledge about the past is like some giant jigsaw puzzle, where the picture gradually fills in, becomes clearer, and is one day complete. A better image is that of a framework that gets steadily bigger. Not only was Stonehenge not built by druids, it was built by many different people over more than a thousand years. A recent study identified 15 distinct 'phases' of work, starting around 3000 BC. We also now know much more about the 'context' of Stonehenge: that the standing stones lie at the heart of a 'ritual landscape' of enclosures, processional ways and burial mounds that stretches for 2 or 3 miles in each direction. So our framework for Stonehenge has expanded – both time-wise and geographically – generating hundreds of new questions for archaeologists. Why was the bluestone circle of Period 2 never finished? Who organized the building of the sarsen circle and trilithons in Period 3? Which of the nearby burial monuments were contemporary with which phases? What religious beliefs underlay such extraordinary effort?

Archaeology, in short, is expanding exponentially. The scale of fieldwork and the number of new discoveries are at an all-time high, and as the body of archaeological data grows, new questions are raised and new lines of research open up. Even so, only a tiny proportion of our archaeological sites have been excavated, and the untapped material potentially available to answer the growing number of questions is truly vast.

Sedgeford is a rural parish in north-west Norfolk. It is the site of a major field project expected to last many years. Each summer, a team of professional archaeologists and several dozen volunteers sets to work to uncover a little more of Sedgeford's past. What is extraordinary is that they cannot keep pace with their own discoveries: they are locating far more buried sites than they are able to dig. Archaeologists use a range of 'non-invasive' techniques that do not disturb the buried remains – studying documents and old maps, looking at aerial photographs, plotting earthworks, fieldwalking and metal-detecting to locate scatters of finds in plough-soil, and various kinds of geophysics to map below-ground 'anomalies'. These methods are finding new sites much faster than the known ones can be excavated. So the tools available for learning about Sedgeford's past are expanding all the time. There are literally dozens of sites in the parish – Bronze Age, Iron Age, Roman, Anglo-Saxon, medieval – that have never been touched by archaeologists. And there is nothing exceptional about Sedgeford. The British landscape is an archaeological treasure-house only a fraction of whose riches has yet been seen.

At the same time, there is terrible destruction – by natural processes like erosion, by quarrying, road-building and urban expansion, and above all by modern farming. In the last 50 years, thousands of archaeological sites have been trashed by the intensification of agriculture – earthworks ploughed flat, waterlogged deposits desiccated by drainage and water-extraction, and the layers representing buried settlements sliced away by deep ploughing, leaving only a scatter of potsherds in the topsoil. Archaeologists are able to investigate only a portion of the sites being lost – mainly those being redeveloped subject to modern planning controls. Even these are rarely excavated in full: usually there are financial resources available only for a 'sampling' of the deposits. In the recent past, the destruction of sites without record has been on an unprecedented scale.

So we have a growing research agenda, a vast body of potential evidence in unexplored archaeological remains, and a fearful rate of uncontrolled destruction. There is work here for an army of amateur archaeologists. Unlike most academic disciplines – which are the work of university specialists in libraries and laboratories – archaeology is driven by discoveries at hundreds of sites scattered across the landscape. Thousands of people are involved in collecting the data. And there is space for thousands more. Nor are the basic techniques difficult. Professionals often like to cloak their skills in mystery to enhance their own prestige, but while there are many high-level skills in archaeology, most of these have been learnt through practice. Everyone started with a set of basics you can pick up in a few days. It is just like any other hobby. If you take up painting, you can produce something that looks a bit like the church on the green the first time you try, but it will take a lot of practice before you have something worth hanging on the wall. No effort, no gain, as in all things. It is the effort – not formal instruction – that is crucial. We all need to be guided as we learn new skills – we need to be instructed in the correct technique – but it is practice and experience that turns knowledge of technique into real skill. Archaeology is like that. Using a metal-detector, laying out a grid for fieldwalking, studying old maps, trowelling the deposits in an excavation trench, recording the timbers of a medieval barn, identifying potsherds or animal bones: these and many other skills are best learnt on site, and most people, within a day or two, can pick up enough to get started, make themselves useful, and begin to enjoy the thrill of uncovering the past.

This book – and the TV series on which it is based – is about metal-detectorists, amateur archaeologists, professional excavators and museum specialists working together to recover the 'hidden treasures' of our heritage. We follow several stories of discovery, and explore what the treasure recovered tells us about a past world. The focus is on the more glamorous discoveries – gold and silver and other rich metalwork – but when it is a peasant's cooking pot, a cheap Viking brooch or the small change from a Roman purse, the excitement of archaeology is there too. Some, after reading the book, may wish to join the search for Britain's past. For those who do, there is plenty of good advice in Chapter 7. In the meantime, here are some splendid stories about ordinary people making spectacular finds. We start with an unclaimed arms cache in east Yorkshire.

TIMELINE

DATE	SOCIETY	SITES	ARTEFACTS
500,000 BC Lower Palaeolithic	Small groups of hunters, scavengers and gatherers *Pre-human hominids*	Boxgrove	Stone hand-axes
150,000 BC Middle Palaeolithic	*Neanderthals*		
35,000 BC Upper Palaeolithic	*Modern humans*		Stone blade tools
8000 BC Mesolithic		Star Carr	Stone microliths for composite tools
3500 BC Neolithic	The agricultural revolution: small groups of farmers	Chambered cairns Long barrows	Polished axes Pottery
2500 BC	Emergence of élite *'Beaker' folk* *Amesbury Archer*	Dartmoor reaves	Beaker pottery Metalworking: copper knives and gold ornaments
2200 BC Early Bronze Age	Developed ruling class	Round barrows Stonehenge: sarsen ring and trilithons erected Seahenge	Bronzeworking: daggers and axes
1900 BC	Wessex culture *Bush Barrow man*	Rich Wessex burials	Grave-goods include gold, bronze, amber, faience and jet **Ringlemere Cup**
1500 BC Late Bronze Age		Hill-forts Sacred sites with ritual deposits of metalwork	
700 BC Early Iron Age			Torcs Decorated military metalwork Chariots La Tène art
100 BC Late Iron Age	Emergence of kings and states *Druids*	Oppida	Gallo-Belgic coins
70 BC			British coins

DATE	SOCIETY	SITES	ARTEFACTS
50 BC	Caesar's expeditions Client-kingship		Inscribed British coins Imported Roman luxuries **Leicestershire coin hoards** **Winchester jewellery hoard**
AD 43 Roman Conquest	Rule by army officers and client-kings *Verica* *Togidubnus*	Forts Folly Lane burial	
Early Roman Britain	Imperial province ruled by Romanized élite	Towns and villas Romano-Celtic temples **Wheathampstead burials** **Sanctuary of Senua**	Frescoes and mosaics Classical art Votive hoards **East Yorkshire** **arms cache**
AD 300 Late Roman Britain	Rule by centralized military state	Decline of towns and villas	
AD 450 Early Anglo- Saxon Period	Small groups of farmers ruled by local chiefs	Cremation and inhumation cemeteries Small settlements with mead-halls and 'SFBs'	Brooches and other decorated metalwork Spears and shields Swords
AD 550	Emergence of early English kingdoms		
	Raedwald and *Wuffingas dynasty*	Sutton Hoo	Early coins: tremisses and thrymsas
AD 650 Middle Anglo- Saxon Period	Developed royal states Highly stratified society	Trading towns Minster churches 'Productive sites' **New site near Ipswich**	Later coins: sceattas **Lincolnshire** **sword handle**
AD 850 Late Anglo- Saxon Period	Struggle between Vikings and Anglo- Saxon kings of Wessex *Alfred the Great*	Burhs: walled towns Viking rural settlements in the Danelaw	Cheap Viking brooches
AD 1066 Norman Conquest	End of Anglo-Saxon England		

1 Discovery! An Unclaimed Arms Cache

Discovery! An Unclaimed Arms Cache

Excitement was building at the regular monthly meeting of the East Yorkshire Metal Detecting Society. Meetings were mainly an opportunity for members to show one another their latest finds and discuss identifications. Among the better preserved finds on display there was the usual rough stuff – small, broken, misshapen, corroded fragments – and less experienced members welcomed the chance to find out more about their discoveries. As well as giving members a chance to see each other's finds, the meeting also featured the society's 'Find of the Month' competition. Three of the members who always went out as a team – Michael Carr, John Connell and Patrick Walby – had put one of their finds on the competition tray late that evening in August 2002. They had not been sure whether to enter it. None of them knew what it was. It comprised a length of copper alloy shaped like a chicken's wishbone, but rather bigger, with lovely mouldings, the whole thing perfectly preserved. They were convinced it was modern – some sort of Victorian fitting perhaps. Nonetheless, at the last minute, it was entered. The tray did the rounds and reached Chris Fenn, the society secretary, who saw the wishbone and did a double take. Chris is a retired design consultant who has spent most of his working life in Dublin but has now returned to his native Hull. Though he started detecting only five years ago, he takes the hobby seriously and is studying archaeology at the local university. He did not know exactly what the wishbone was – a plough had opened it out so it looked like a spur – but he was pretty certain he knew its date. The decoration was 'diagnostic': it was in a style that tied the object to a particular period. What was amazing was its preservation: it looked completely fresh, as if it had been made yesterday.

'Hold on, lads. This is most definitely Iron Age. The decoration is distinctly La Tène. This isn't just the find of the month. It's the find of the year.'

Once you have got your eye in, La Tène is so distinctive that you tend to recognize it when you see it. Chris was ahead of most of the members, and there was a lot of scepticism. It looked as if a bit of Victorian rubbish was going to bag the prize.

Chris had a quiet word with the three finders. Mike, John and Pat – experienced though they were, having had some excellent finds on other sites – were keen to follow advice. They trusted Chris, who seemed to know his stuff, and they were persuaded to go back to the find-spot and have another look. Whatever it was they had, it looked like a piece broken off a larger object. A few days later, Chris got a phone call around six o'clock in the evening. Though it was a weekday and rain had been bucketing down since early that morning, the three had gone back to the site after work and started detecting near the original find-spot. They had found something almost straight away. About 2 yards from where the first find had come up, John

Left: The mystery object found by John Connell, with its distinctive 'La Tène' detail – the stylized head of a bird or beast on either side. It could be dated to the Iron Age – but what is it?

received a very strong ferrous signal. He called the other two over to check the target with their machines, and they confirmed it was something big and iron. But was it worth digging?

Discovering a Hidden World

One of the great myths about metal-detectorists – not least among professional archaeologists – is that they are digging up undisturbed hoards of deeply buried treasure. The truth is rather different: 90 per cent of recorded finds come from cultivated land and, because most metal-detectors cannot pick up small objects more than a few inches down, the vast bulk of these are from plough-soil. That is why collections of metal-detected finds often look so rough. They have been yanked from their original resting place by the deep-cutting, fast-moving blades of a motorized plough. Once in the plough-soil, they get this treatment on a regular basis. They also become more exposed to air and rain, and they get dowsed with highly corrosive chemical fertilizers. Older detectorists have even noticed a deterioration during their 20 or 30 years in the hobby: you can see the effects more deep ploughing and more chemical inputs have had on the finds. Modern agriculture is the single greatest destroyer of our buried heritage. When it takes off a fresh slice of archaeology, sprinkling new artefacts through the plough-soil, these objects have been moved on to death row. After a few years, most of them will be unrecognizable bits of corrosion. Their only chance of a reprieve is to be salvaged by a metal-detector.

Although Britain's arable land is full of metal, most of it is modern rubbish, mainly nails, but also including large lumps of rusty iron from recent agriculture, like horseshoes, bits of tractor chain and broken ploughshares. A recent survey of a field to test the proportion of ferrous to non-ferrous metalwork in plough-soil found that 98 per cent of finds were iron and 75 per cent of those were nails. So most detectorists want to avoid iron.

They do this by setting the 'discriminator' on their machines to 'knock out' ferrous finds. This requires a little explanation. The search head of a metal-detector contains a transmitter and antennae which generate a ground-penetrating electro-magnetic field. Metal objects in the ground disrupt that field and create a localized disturbance that can be picked up by the antennae and amplified by the detector's circuitry. This disturbance is then turned into an audio or visual signal that the operator receives either through headphones or by observing the monitor on the machine's control-box. However, different metals have

La Tène Decoration

La Tène is the name given to a style of decoration used by the Celtic Iron Age peoples of north and west Europe from the fifth century BC to the second century AD. Curving geometric motifs and stylized plants and animals are woven into intricate designs of circles and loops that flow across the surfaces of bronze artefacts. The name 'La Tène' comes from the lakeside site in Switzerland where the style was first recognized in the late nineteenth century.

different conductivity and therefore disrupt the electro-magnetic field in different ways. The discriminator exploits this to allow the operator to knock out certain signals.

Iron is highly conductive and gives strong signals, so you can set the machine to exclude much of it. But there are limits. The discriminator can be set to exclude objects ranging from, at one extreme, small iron nails to, at the other, aluminium ring pulls. Most detectorists set it close to the bottom of the range because anything higher risks losing finds. There is a 'safe level' for the discriminator so as not to exclude the weak signals given off by small non-ferrous objects lying at depth. But at the safe level, some iron is bound to come through. The bigger an object and the closer to the surface it is, the stronger the signal. If you want to detect a small silver coin 4 inches down, you will probably also hear a large iron nail at the same depth, or an iron ploughshare at twice the depth.

Nowadays, though, you almost always know if a signal is from iron. Many machines have built-in monitors that give provisional IDs and an estimated depth. Experienced detectorists, anyway, can tell from the tones in the headphones. They talk about 'going into their own little world' when they put the headphones on and focus on the sounds.

Mike, John and Pat knew they had something that was big, deep and ferrous. A lot of detectorists would have ignored it. But the signal here was even bigger than you usually get with modern rubbish, and Chris had insisted they were on to something. So they dug a small hole and had a look. They then hit something completely unexpected – instead of iron 15 inches down, they had copper alloy at 5 inches. As they dug down around it, they could see it was a large object that dived away vertically. It was at least a foot long, but the part they could see had been bent upright and the rest of it was lying horizontally and running underneath the side of the hole. A plough must have snagged on the end and pulled it upwards. But there was not just one object. They could see another lying beside the first one, at the base of the hole – and a big chunk of thick-walled pottery. There are people who would have dug it all out quickly, yanking at the objects if they had not come readily, completing the destruction already begun by the plough. Instead, Mike, John and Pat, in a state of growing excitement, decided to call Chris Fenn and ask him to come down.

It was not yet dark and the rain had stopped, so Chris readily agreed to visit the site immediately – as long as the guys were happy about that. Detectorists tend to be secretive about sites within their clubs. What they do not want is other members pestering farmers to get onto a site where they are already working. So finds are in the public domain, but locations are kept confidential. Though Chris was the club secretary, he did not know where the three had been working. Rather than him getting lost trying to find the field, they arranged to meet him at a local post office. So, with a hurriedly made flask of tea and packet of sandwiches, Chris set off in his car on a 20-minute drive to a slightly surreal rendezvous in the east Yorks countryside. He felt privileged. It was his identification, his hunch there was something big, that had encouraged his colleagues to go back to the site, and now they had reciprocated by letting him in on it.

Driving on from the post office, they soon reached the site. The find-spot was quite close to the hedge-line in a field that sloped gently upwards to a line of trees. When Mike, John and Pat pulled back the cover they had put over the hole, Chris was awe-struck. He was looking at two decorated La Tène sword scabbards that no one had seen for 2,000 years. It was apparent that the original 'wishbone' was a sword chape: the sides had got splayed out, but originally they had been parallel and had fitted neatly on to the end of a scabbard. Swords were weapons of the Iron Age aristocracy. They were finely crafted, highly decorated, and treasured as items of great value. To find one is a once-in-a-lifetime discovery, and here there were at least two. Chris knew what needed to be done and, as he said, 'The guys were brilliant about it': they accepted that it was a major discovery and that the objects, although hit by the plough, were still *in situ* – which meant the archaeologists needed to be called in.

Below: Two of the beautifully decorated La Tène scabbards as they slowly emerge from the soil for the first time in 2,000 years.

The Experts Arrive

The following morning there was another rendezvous at the post office. Dave Evans, the head of Humber Archaeology Partnership, had got a call from Chris first thing. Within the hour he had arrived with a team of three archaeologists. When they got to the site they started work immediately, gently trowelling around the artefacts to expose them fully. As they did so, they found more. There were not two but three Iron Age swords, each with an elaborate handle and a beautifully decorated La Tène scabbard. Beside them lay a bundle of around a dozen, 2-foot-long, socketed iron spearheads. Overlying both sets of weapons were the big chunky sherds of a broken Roman amphora – a type of ceramic storage vessel used for transporting wine and oil. It was clear that all the damage – the chape ripped off, the scabbard bent back, the smashed amphora – was the result of one or more blows by the plough.

The situation required extreme sensitivity. The artefacts were large, close-packed, made of composite materials, and covered in well-preserved but delicate decoration – 'repoussé' designs punched into the metal, applied bronze strips, blue glass insets, evidence of gilding in places, a sword handle that appeared to be made of carved antler with metal bindings and inlaid enamel or coral at the extremities. Exposing the upper surfaces was only the first of several potentially hazardous operations. Each artefact then had to be separated from those it was touching without causing damage, bound up to prevent it falling apart, and lifted out of the ground in one piece. Digging up stuff like this is not routine. Walls, ditches, pits, spreads of hardcore, rubbish dumps, scatters of broken potsherds and animal bones: this is the norm. A single sword might be the best thing an archaeologist gets to dig in his or her career – but here was a whole cache of top-grade weaponry. The excavators needed specialist advice, so Dave Evans called in a team of conservators from the York Archaeological Trust, who arrived that evening.

What was the condition of the artefacts? What materials were involved? What special treatments or procedures might be needed? In dealing with delicate finds in the field there are always three main issues. One is the need to avoid causing damage in the digging process itself. This is mainly a matter of going slowly, using light tools and exercising care. The second issue is much more tricky and requires specialist knowledge. Many archaeological artefacts decay when buried in the ground. The form and rate of decay vary according to the type of material and the local soil and climatic conditions. Where the burial environment remains unchanged for long periods, the process of decay might slow

and almost stop. Established layers of corrosion often provide a barrier to further attack by the agents of decay – water, oxygen and chemicals in the soil. The artefact becomes stable. Excavation destroys the burial environment and changes the conditions around the artefact abruptly. A rapid

Above: Lisa Wasling (left), senior finds officer, with Erica Patterson (centre) and Lisa Veere-Stephens (right) excavating the hoard. Each sword and scabbard requires hours of painstaking work by archaeologists and conservators.

process of renewed decay can then set in. What is urgently needed at that point is 'first aid for finds': action that will stabilize the material temporarily until full conservation in the lab is possible. The third issue is also one for the specialist: the wrapping, lifting and transport of what may be physically fragile and chemically unstable objects made of composite materials. A good excavator is not someone who knows how to do all this; it is someone who knows when to call in the people who do. Dave had the conservators on site before the end of the first day.

The first sword took nearly two days. First it had to be fully exposed by gentle trowelling and brushing, and then recorded *in situ* with a scale drawing, photographs and a set of written notes. It was then wrapped, fitted into a tray for support, lifted clear of the trench, labelled and made ready for transportation. Every time an artefact was removed, care was taken to collect up any loose fragments, each of which was separately bagged and labelled. Samples of surrounding soil were taken for chemical analysis to help with conservation decisions. With the first artefacts lifted, the estimate of the size of the cache had to be revised upwards again: not two, not three, but *five* Iron Age swords. The whole excavation took a week. In that time – 'a week of non-stop excitement in red-hot weather' according to Chris Fenn – a strong bond developed between the amateur metal-detectorists and the professional archaeologists. Everyone helped out with the excavation, and Mike and John, fearing word might have got out, slept in their car each night to guard the site. They came to understand why archaeologists hate 'nighthawks' so much. This time it was *their* site that was under threat if someone should hear of it before the excavation was finished.

Thieves in the Night

Nighthawks are crooks equipped with metal-detectors who go on to archaeological sites at night and loot antiquities to sell on the black market. They are in it for the money. They do not give a toss about a heritage that belongs to everyone. Hard facts about nighthawking are few – criminals do not advertise their achievements – but the Council for British Archaeology tried to find out what it could in a survey in the early 1990s. One finding was that over a five-year period there was definite evidence for attacks on 188 scheduled ancient monuments (major sites under government protection); and, since many monuments are not closely monitored and nighthawking often leaves few traces, this figure is a bare minimum. They also found that 37 out of 50 professional units had suffered raids on their excavation sites. Museum staff at Corbridge, the Roman military base near Hadrian's Wall, had been especially vigilant. They estimated at least 23 raids over a four-year period, some of them highly organized, which took place shortly after ploughing when the soil was freshly turned, with up to ten people walking regular lines at 15-foot intervals.

Evidence from elsewhere was more impressionistic, but local archaeologists reckoned that raids on the greenfield Roman town site of Caistor-by-Norwich in Norfolk, for instance, had sometimes averaged one a week. What was clear was that nighthawking was – and remains – a major threat to everyone's archaeological heritage. It is the tacky end of an illegal trade that runs through well-heeled dealers and respectable auction houses to rich private collectors who hoard looted antiquities for their own amusement. That is why the government is currently backing a private member's bill to make dealing in looted antiquities a criminal offence.

When the dig was finished, before leaving the site for the last time the archaeologists went over to the detectorists, shook their hands and thanked them. It was one of those slightly embarrassing moments when something has to be said and everyone feels a bit emotional. It had been quite a week. Metal-detectorists and archaeologists do not always get on. There are still some archaeologists around who regard all detectorists as looters. But these were three ordinary guys who had saved a hoard of Iron Age weaponry from the plough and called in a team of archaeologists to make sure it was dug properly. So it was important to say something.

'Perhaps only once in your career as an archaeologist,' said Dave Evans, 'do you get a chance to be involved with something as significant as this. Thanks for bringing us in on it.'

What Does It All Mean?

The final reckoning was 5 swords (with ornate handles), 5 scabbards (all with superb La Tène decoration), 34 spearheads in a tight bundle and the remains of a big, globular Roman amphora of a type used for transporting oil. Chris Fenn's press statement was effusive: 'The swords display the very highest levels of the Celtic bronzesmith's art and craftsmanship: their design and intricate decoration, and the quality and combination of materials used, show them to be the weapons of a warrior élite in Late Iron Age society. They would have been custom-built, symbols of power and authority, and more likely ceremonial than utilitarian in nature. All five are of what is known as "the northern style", and they may well have been tribal or family heirlooms, already of some age before their deposition, since Roman pottery was found beneath them in the boundary ditch in which they lay.'

His enthusiasm was not misplaced. The experts were stunned. Peter Addyman of the York Archaeological Trust likened the find to 'discovering a Picasso in your loft', Kevin Leahy of North Lincolnshire Museum declared, 'The Iron Age does not get any better than this', and Iron Age weapons specialist Ian Stead announced the hoard to be unique. Nowhere in Celtic Europe, it seems, had five decorated bronze scabbards ever been found

together like this, and fewer than ten Iron Age swords had previously been found anywhere in northern England.

What were they doing here? No one yet knows. Dave Evans's team had established that they lay within a shallow boundary ditch amid a dump of domestic rubbish (broken pottery and animal bones). The British Museum's J.D. Hill has confirmed that the swords are of the 'northern' or 'Brigantian' type (the Brigantes being the local Iron Age tribe). These artefacts are found only in northern England and southern Scotland and, while wholly Celtic in style, actually date to the Early Roman period (later first and second centuries AD). This fits the pottery evidence at the find-spot. The swords had been placed in a pit that cut into the fill of an earlier ditch containing Roman pottery. And the broken amphora on top of the swords was of a type rarely found before the Roman Conquest in AD 43, but common thereafter up to c AD 260. Were these the illegal weapons of local hill-tribesmen? Had they belonged to raiders from the unconquered north? Or were they the legitimate arms of British auxiliaries enrolled in the Roman army? Why were they stashed here? Had they been buried for safety, or were they an offering to the gods? There is a natural spring a short distance away, and the farmer reports an area of the field where his plough regularly hits something solid. Is it a pagan temple to a water deity?

The story of Mike, John and Pat's 'unclaimed arms cache' is unfinished. The British Museum may acquire the artefacts, but if it does, the conservators there will need to do thousands of pounds' worth of work before they can be put on public display. If money is

available and the landowner willing, the area around the find-spot may be explored to answer some of the questions thrown up by the hoard. It is the usual story of a fresh discovery enlarging the framework

of knowledge and creating new gaps. 'More research is needed,' as archaeologists are forever saying.

The seven stories that follow are of discoveries that are further down the road of research. In these, the work of metal-detectorists has been followed by field surveys and excavations; and the finds have been given a geographical context, a place in an ancient landscape, so that they can tell a fuller story. They become portals into lost worlds. A golden goblet first transports us back 3,500 years to the Early Bronze Age and an encounter with Britain's first ruling class (Chapter 2). A field of coins and two sets of golden jewellery then take us to the Late Iron Age and a world of druids, warrior lords and Celtic kings (Chapter 3). The fine bronze pitchers from two graves show us the aristocracy of Roman Britain, and a stash of gold and silver offerings introduces us to the mysterious Romano-Celtic goddess Senua (Chapter 4). Coins, brooches and belt-buckles from a field in Suffolk, and a golden sword handle from another in Lincolnshire, give us entry to the Anglo-Saxon mead-halls of the seventh century AD (Chapter 5). Then we look briefly at how hundreds of cheap trinkets are revealing the Viking settlers of the tenth century (Chapter 6), before concluding with advice on ways to join the search for Britain's 'hidden treasure' (Chapter 7).

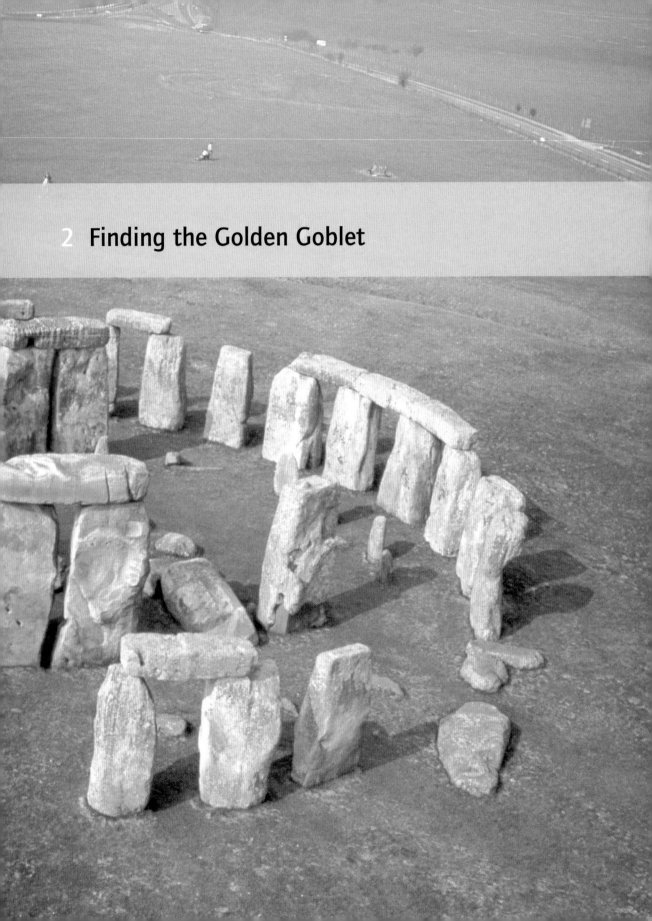

2 Finding the Golden Goblet

Finding the Golden Goblet

Cliff Bradshaw, a retired electrician, makes no claim to be an 'expert', but, like many veteran detectorists, experience has given him a feel for ancient landscape. In November 2001 all the fields where he usually worked were under crop, so one Saturday two fellow-detectorists invited him to help out on one of theirs.

Cliff knew straight away that this field was a good site. Though there was a mix of stuff coming off it – Iron Age, Roman, medieval – it was the Early Anglo-Saxon that stood out. There is always a certain amount of 'background noise': a Roman brooch accidentally dropped by a passer-by, a medieval coin lost in the farmyard manure, the musket balls of eighteenth-century sportsmen. One trinket does not make a site. But the quantity of Anglo-Saxon finds, including a couple of coins and some fragments of brooch, was well above normal. Then Cliff noticed a slightly raised rectangle of ground – the right sort of size for a building platform – and within half an hour of starting to detect across this he had four spindle-whorls (used in spinning wool into thread) and a silver strap-end (perhaps from a belt). He was now certain this was an Early Anglo-Saxon settlement site. If so, there would almost certainly be a cemetery nearby – a pagan cemetery full of metal grave-goods.

Above: Hidden Treasure *presenter Miranda Krestovnikoff with Cliff Bradshaw, finder of the Ringlemere Cup.*

'I scanned the horizon,' Cliff recalls, 'and then I saw the mound.' *The* mound. It was late autumn, the vegetation was down, and they were in an open countryside of huge ploughed fields where earthworks, if anything at all survived, showed up well. This one was slight but most definitely there: a foot or so of raised earth that extended across an area about the size of a tennis court. 'I walked over to it and started detecting. I had soon found a gilded Anglo-Saxon button-brooch, and that convinced me I was on a cemetery site. But I had run out of time that day. It would have to wait until tomorrow.'

On the Sunday morning, Cliff first stood in what seemed to be the centre of the mound. Knowing this would be the deepest part – and that his detector would be unlikely to pick up anything buried there – he went to the edge of the mound and started detecting his way around the perimeter. On perhaps the second circuit, he got a minute signal. Maybe something, but it was at the absolute limit of the machine's capacity. He scraped the ground with his foot and tried again. The signal was still very faint, but the sound had increased. There *was* something, though deep. Several times, now using the specialized mini-spade he carried, he dug away the earth and tested again with the detector, gradually closing in on the target, digging away on either side of it to avoid damaging it. He knew it was not iron because instead of a low growl the machine was giving off a high-pitched whine: that meant something non-ferrous. What was odd was that the audio signal and the meter reading were out of sync: normally with a tin can – the most likely non-ferrous 'discovery' – the audio screams at you and the meter goes off the scale. This time the meter was stuck on the half-way mark. So maybe it was something else.

The Gleam of Gold

Well over a foot down, Cliff saw it for the first time. Whatever it was, it was gold. The astonishing thing about gold is that it is stunningly beautiful the moment you uncover it. Silver looks purple-grey, bronze goes green, and iron turns into shapeless rusty lumps. Not so gold: there is no corrosion, no discoloration, just the same brilliant yellow gleam it had when its owner last saw it hundreds or even thousands of years before. Because it is highly visible, it is easily excavated, and Cliff took little time to expose the object fully and lift it out. The first thing he noticed was a savage dent that had crumpled the object on one side, and he had the momentary fear that somehow, despite his care he had, without realizing, dug into it with his spade. But he knew this had not happened; and this was a potato field – it supplied the local fish and chip shops – and modern potato cultivation means

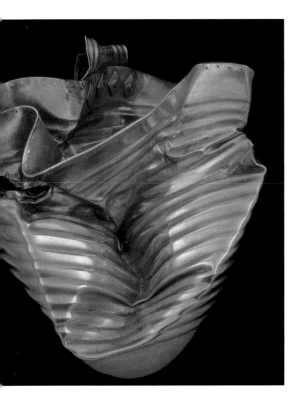

Left: The Ringlemere Cup, its gleam of gold undiminished after 3,500 years in the ground.

motorized blades cutting 18 inches deep. The object had clearly been struck hard, yanked from its resting place and pulled some distance through the ground. Made of sheet-gold no thicker than light cardboard, it was now within the range of a plough and if Cliff had not recovered it, it would gradually have been destroyed. Detectorists like Cliff are salvage archaeologists.

He held in his hand a fragile, beautiful, mysterious object. It was clearly a cup, about the size of a coffee mug, with thin corrugated sides, punched dots beneath the rim, a rounded base, and a delicate little handle attached by rivets secured with lozenge-shaped washers. Cliff should have been excited – ecstatic even – at what was obviously the find of a lifetime. Some people would have thought about the money: how much would they get? In fact, most detectorists never become rich, and are not in metal-detecting to get rich: it is the history that they love. Cliff was neither particularly excited nor thinking about value. Instead he was obsessed by the thought that it did not look Anglo-Saxon – and if not that, then what? It was only as he was driving home that he remembered he had seen a picture of a very similar object. But where?

A few days later Keith Parfitt, the leading Dover archaeologist, got a phone call. Keith knew, and had worked with, many of the local detectorists but he had never met Cliff Bradshaw, who phoned him out of the blue, having seen him doing his stuff at a couple of lectures.

'I think I've found a gold cup from the Bronze Age. It's like one I've got a picture of in a book.'

Keith thought for a moment and then asked, 'You mean the Rillaton Cup?'

'I can't remember the name. Hang on a minute. I'll check.'

The Rillaton Cup was unique: the only example of a gold cup of Early Bronze Age date ever discovered in Britain. It had been found in a burial cairn in Cornwall by early nineteenth-century workmen, and was now proudly displayed in the British Museum's prehistory gallery. No one had found one since.

'Yes,' said the voice on the end of the phone, 'it's like the Rillaton Cup.'

Keith had been an archaeologist for many years and was used to members of the public who got over-enthusiastic about their finds – not to mention the occasional outright crank. He accepted that this caller had found something, but he did not believe the identification. 'I could tell from his voice that he didn't believe me,' recalls Cliff, 'but I was pretty sure about it, so I sent him some photos.'

When the photos arrived the next morning, Keith Parfitt discovered that the Rillaton Cup was no longer unique. Cliff Bradshaw had found another one.

Bronze Age Burials

Cliff had found a portal into a world much, much older than his Anglo-Saxon settlement. The Ringlemere Cup – as it came to be known – had already been in the ground 2,000 years by that period. The mound that contained it was probably revered by the Anglo-Saxons: they were pagans, steeped in Germanic myths of gods and heroes, easily able to imagine such places as ancient tombs. They often chose to bury their own dead around them, and Cliff had found that Early Anglo-Saxon button-brooch nearby – perhaps a deposit from a grave destroyed by a plough. But what of the gold cup? Had it come from the tomb of a Bronze Age chieftain?

When Keith Parfitt brought in a team of volunteer diggers from the Dover Archaeological Group they drew something of a blank. Though the mound had not been ploughed completely flat – as so many are – the little that remained was so disturbed that no trace of any burial could be found in the area where the cup had been found. Had there been one, it might have been spectacular. Not only was there the golden cup, there was also the sheer size of the mound: more than 150 feet across, making it one of the biggest round-barrows in Britain. Enclosed by a massive ditch, it may once have risen 15 or 20 feet high: a monumental feature in the Bronze Age landscape, and the burial place (if such it was) of

a person of high rank – or several such persons over successive generations, for barrows, like the mausolea of great families, often contain secondary burials. The gold cup need not have come from a primary burial at the centre of the mound. The

Above: Not quite what they were looking for - Keith Parfitt's team finds a dagger's pommel in this unidentified circular feature, but no evidence for a great Bronze Age burial.

Rillaton Cup had come from a cist – a stone-lined burial chamber – dug into an existing cairn. (Piles of stones – or 'cairns' – were used in the same way in upland areas as earth mounds – or 'barrows' – in the lowlands.) Lying in the cist had been the body of a man and, as well as the cup, a ceramic pot, a set of beads and a fine bronze dagger. Perhaps the missing Ringlemere man had also had a dagger – though there was no sign of a blade, Keith Parfitt's team found the end of a pommel made from amber in the spoil from the dig.

A gold cup, a huge mound, a fancy dagger: altogether there were clues enough from Ringlemere to place the site in context. Between about 2200 and 1500 BC, during what archaeologists call 'the Early Bronze Age', a fair proportion of graves contained objects of gold – earrings, pendants, 'spacers' on necklaces, belt-fittings, decorations on dagger handles, and the like. Most spectacular of all was a golden cape found around the shoulders of a skeleton buried in a stone cist beneath a cairn at Mold in Flintshire. It is now a prize exhibit among the Bronze Age artefacts on display in the British Museum. As well as occasional items of gold, the richer graves might also contain exotic objects made from amber (fossilized resin imported from the Baltic), faience (a form of blue glass invented in the East), jet (a shiny black stone from north Yorkshire that could be carved and polished) or, of course, bronze (an alloy of nine parts copper to one part tin). Accompanying objects of cheaper material like pottery (perhaps a little 'incense cup') or stone (perhaps a polished axe-head) would still be finely crafted. For posh burials in the Early Bronze Age there was, then, a cultural 'package': a standard range of status symbols from which a selection could be made. Similar objects recur, albeit in slightly different combinations, the fashions changing only slowly over the centuries. To choose objects from this range – to treasure them and place them reverentially in the grave alongside one's dead – was to make a statement of membership, of shared identity, of solidarity with others who also chose such objects.

This is what archaeologists mean by a 'culture': a set of typical objects from a specific time that can be read as evidence for the existence in the past of a community of people somehow bound together. Thus we describe the richest graves of Early Bronze Age Britain as belonging to the 'Wessex culture', and we further distinguish between an early and a late flowering of this culture – 'Wessex I' in c1900–1700 BC and 'Wessex II' in c1700–1500 BC. Ringlemere, Rillaton and Mold are in fact outliers of a

Left: An artist's impression of an Early Bronze Age lord of the so-called 'Wessex culture'. The wealth of their grave-goods marks them out as members of Britain's first ruling class.

type of burial mainly centred on the chalk downs of Salisbury Plain in south-central England. Round-barrows cluster especially around the famous stone circles at Avebury and Stonehenge; within a 2-mile radius of the latter there are more than 260. Of these Wessex burials, about a hundred are known from excavation to have been rich in grave-goods. The richest of them all was opened in 1808.

The treasure-hunters then were country gentlemen of antiquarian interests and ample means. Foremost among them 200 years ago was Sir Richard Colt Hoare, baronet, landowner and banker, who employed his friend, the wool merchant Mr William Cunnington, to supervise teams of workmen digging the barrows around Stonehenge. Cunnington's greatest discovery was the burial inside Bush Barrow.

It was a small mound less than a mile south of the Stones that looked like an inverted bowl. Its modest appearance gave no clue to the riches within. Excavation revealed the skeleton of a well-built man lying stretched out on his back. With him in the grave were two lozenge-shaped plates of sheet-gold that had once adorned his clothing; a bronze axe-head; a gold plate with a hook that had been fitted to a belt or scabbard; three daggers, two of bronze, the third of copper with a gold-studded pommel; and a polished stone mace-head, possibly a sceptre since its handle had been fitted with cylindrical bone mounts. Who was the Bush Barrow man? Who were the others buried with such peculiar pomp in Early Bronze Age Britain?

A thousand years before, in the Neolithic or New Stone Age, before the coming of metals, people had been buried in large collective tombs – long barrows or chambered cairns – their bones laid to rest without grave-goods alongside those of their ancestors. This was the way of death in the classless world of early farmers. Death mirrors life, and all bones were equal in the intimacy of the long barrow. But centuries before the Wessex culture flourished, the entrance passages of the collective tombs had been blocked up, and single burial in round-barrows or cairns became the norm. Some 30,000 of these monuments are known in Britain, usually grouped in cemeteries of anything from four to 40 mounds. The individual mattered now, and some, judged by the grandeur of the monuments or the richness of the goods within them, mattered much more than others. The noble dead were dispatched with symbols of their status, equipped to resume their proper place at the head of society when they reached the Other Side. The round-barrow cemeteries of Wessex were the burial places of Britain's first ruling class.

We cannot name any of them, of course, for they sleep for ever in what one eminent

Above: Sunrise at Stonehenge, an Early Bronze Age temple for the worship of the sun and the spirits of the ancestors.

archaeologist called 'the grey night of remote prehistory'. The earliest Briton whose name has survived belongs to the first century BC. Nor can we reconstruct political events in Bronze Age Britain. Without written sources, with only monuments, artefacts and bones, we are reduced to generalities and conjectures. Even so, peering into the darkness, we can perhaps see the shadowy forms of chieftains, priests and warriors. The Bush Barrow man was once imagined to have been the architect of Stonehenge. Though a whimsical idea, it is a reminder that the monument was massively reconstructed in stone in the late third millennium BC – right at the start of the Early Bronze Age.

The Meaning of Stonehenge

The Avenue – a 2-mile processional way linking Stonehenge with the river Avon – was marked out by the digging of two parallel ditches. At the monument itself, an unfinished circle formed of 82 undressed bluestones was erected, each one up to 4 tons in weight, having been transported 135 miles from the Presceli mountains in south Wales. It has been estimated that it took about 360,000 person-hours to construct. Probably a full circle was intended, but it was never completed, for another wholesale remodelling of the sanctuary was soon under way. Massive sarsen stones, the heaviest weighing almost 30 tons, were hauled overland from the Marlborough Downs 24 miles away. Thirty dressed sarsens topped by lintels were then erected to form a continuous ring, while inside the ring were placed five massive, free-standing trilithons (two uprights and a lintel) arranged in a horseshoe shape. The labour cost was perhaps 1,750,000 person-hours. The whole reconstructed complex, like its earth-and-timber precursors, was oriented on the rising midsummer sun. This does not mean Stonehenge was an 'astronomical observatory'; rather, almost certainly, it was a temple for worshipping the sun – the supreme god, perhaps, of light, fertility and the renewal of life in the Early Bronze Age. The high priests, in reconstructing the sun god's temple on such a monumental scale, reveal themselves to us not only as men of great piety, but also as men of immense power, able to command the labour of thousands.

We do not know what a high priest's grave looked like in the Early Bronze Age. Perhaps it was no different from the grave of a chieftain or warrior. Many societies combine these roles: druids (Celtic priests of the Iron Age) could be chieftains, armour-clad bishops fought in medieval battles and the formal head of the Church of England has always been the British monarch. So the roles of priest, ruler and soldier might well have been fused in the Early Bronze Age. Certainly, when laid to rest in their graves, we see virtually all high-ranking men kitted out as warriors. The Bronze Age world was a violent one, and the panoply of the warrior – including arms and armour of expensive metal – was the preserve of an élite. Rank was expressed in military display. Early in our period, in the late third millennium BC, the so-called 'Amesbury Archer' was buried near Avebury with several pottery drinking cups, three copper knives, a quiver full of arrows, and two stone wrist-guards to protect his left arm from the whiplash of the bowstring. Several centuries later, the Bush Barrow man, with his axe and daggers, was surely a warrior, while his gold plates and ceremonial mace-sceptre must place him among the chieftains or high priests. These lords of the Wessex culture remain the most shadowy of figures, but studying their grave-goods and reading these as statements about rank and identity we can make out something of the form of this prehistoric ruling class. Where, however, did such unprecedented wealth and power come from?

The Sources of Bronze Age Wealth

It is hard to know where to look to find out. The Bronze Age landscapes around Avebury and Stonehenge are exceptional, both because they were places of ritual and burial, not everyday life, and because they have survived so well. Elsewhere, enclosures and ploughing have erased most traces of the ancient landscape. The foot or so of mound at Ringlemere in Kent is a rare remnant for south-east England. 'What has happened to Britain's upstanding Bronze Age remains?' asks Caroline Malone, a leading prehistorian. 'They have been trashed continually since the earliest conquests of the island, and 40 per cent of what was left in 1946 has now been levelled by modern agriculture. So it is hardly surprising we see next to nothing. That's why we need detectorists like Cliff to find the last few fragments from an illustrious past – before the plough destroys the evidence completely.' Here and there a tiny stretch of Bronze Age boundary might be fossilized in a sunken lane or ancient hedgerow – but rarely do we realize it and, even if we do, it is but a fragment. Only in a few remote spots do entire Bronze Age landscapes of boundaries, fields, trackways, farmyards and peasant houses still survive. The upland heaths of Dartmoor in Devon are one such place. In the 1970s and 1980s, Andrew Fleming surveyed and recorded a huge network of drystone walls – called 'reaves' – which enclosed large rectangular fields and sometimes ran for miles. They had been thought of as medieval; Andrew Fleming showed that they were Bronze Age and the result of a massive campaign of land clearance at that time. Some trees were removed as early as 4000 BC, but around 2500 BC there were further clearances, and by about 1500 BC virtually the whole of the moor was under cultivation. During this time, the land filled with people – up to 30 per square mile on one estimate. Across Dartmoor, hundreds of isolated farmsteads and tiny hamlets survive

Right: The visible remains of one of the 24 huts of the Grimspound settlement on Dartmoor in Devon, thought to be occupied during the Bronze Age.

from the Bronze Age. Each was once a group of small, circular, stone huts with conical roofs of thatch – home to a family, or perhaps even a handful of families linked by blood and marriage. Saddle-querns for grinding flour attest cereal production. Spindle-whorls and loom-weights attest animal husbandry. These were tiny farming settlements that raised crops, reared animals and lived close to subsistence. But almost certainly they produced a

small surplus above basic needs, and this, or most of it, was paid in tribute to their rulers. Control over land and labour within an expanding agricultural domain was surely one source of wealth for an Early Bronze Age aristocracy.

More land under cultivation, an expanding population, a growing surplus to enrich a few: here is cause enough for the wars implied by the battle-gear with which the Wessex lords were buried. There is evidence, too, for a division of the land into tribal territories, each one focused on its own henge monument and cluster of barrows. Groups of standing stones and cairns are still common survivals in the British uplands, and the spectacular discovery off the north Norfolk coast in 1998 of 'Seahenge', a small timber circle enclosing an inverted oak trunk dated 2050 BC, is a welcome reminder of a ritual landscape otherwise largely lost in the heavily cultivated lowlands. Detailed survey in the upper Thames valley has revealed clusters of ploughed-out barrows every 2 miles or so; in the Great Ouse valley it is every 6 miles. Do these distances perhaps indicate typical sizes for tribal territories ruled by their own chiefs in Bronze Age Britain? Are the barrows claims to power and territory by rival clan-chiefs? In Wessex itself there may have been four or five such territories, perhaps combined in some loose confederation, and perhaps claiming some overarching sovereignty over southern Britain as a whole – much as Homer's Agamemnon, the ruler of 'golden Mycenae', was the leader of all the Greek chieftains who fought at Troy.

The poetic world of *The Iliad* and *The Odyssey* may contain pale reflections of real worlds like that in Britain in 2200–1500 BC. Like the Wessex lords, Homer's heroes were also Bronze Age warriors. Agamemnon ruled not by force, but by uneasy consent. His barons were not so much royal subjects as 'guest friends' – they had a place at his table, spoke their minds in council and shared in the distribution of booty. Relationships were cemented through ritualized 'gift exchange'. When the wandering Odysseus announced his departure from the palace of King Alkinoös, his host knew the etiquette. 'Now I lay this charge upon each man of you,' he declared to his assembled retainers, 'such as here in my palace drink the gleaming wine of the princes always at my side, and hear the song of the singer. Clothing for our guest is stored away in the polished chest, and intricately wrought gold, and all those other gifts the Phaiakian men of counsel brought here to give him. Come, let us man by man each one of us give a great tripod and a cauldron, and we will make it good to us by a collection among the people.' A whole social order is revealed here – of aristocratic warriors bound together by ties of hospitality and present-giving, and of a subject class of peasants from whom their wealth is drawn.

Left: A typical pottery vessel in the 'Beaker' style of the late third millennium BC.
Below: The Rillaton Cup.

The wine flowed freely in Homer's world of heroes. Bonds between men were strengthened as they boozed and feasted together round the lord's hearth. Drinking sets are typical grave-goods in many barbarian warrior cultures. Is this the meaning of the cups in Wessex graves? The Amesbury Archer was buried with his ceramic containers and drinking-cups. These were in a distinctive 'Beaker' style, a type widely distributed across Britain and Europe at the time – but it may have been the contents rather than the vessels that were really being traded. Lime pollen was found where liquid had spilled from such a beaker in a grave near Fife in Scotland – evidence that the liquid was mead, an alcoholic drink made from fermented lime honey and flavoured with meadowsweet. Later, in the richer graves at least, drinking vessels were made of shale, amber or even gold – and Caroline Malone can see a line of such cups in graves extending across southern Britain, linking Rillaton in Cornwall with Ringlemere in Kent, as she explains:

Beakers a few hundred years earlier were about drinking and perhaps the consumption of alcohol. It was men only. And it was a drinking élite. Many traditional societies see getting drunk as linked with special status. The cups seem a logical continuation of this. And the wealth that these cups represent suggest that a major trade route ran along the whole of southern Britain – and over to the Continent, where three other gold cups have been found. And the heart of the trade was tin – Cornish tin – without which the Bronze Age in much of Europe could not have happened. The trade in tin would have made some people very rich indeed. Rich enough to commission, and be buried with, gold cups.

Metals were central to the Bronze Age economy. Gold for the classy trinkets that cemented alliances. Copper and tin for the armaments that won territory. The gold in Early Bronze Age graves may have come from Cornwall, Wales or, more likely, Ireland. Even if the Wessex lords did not control production, they stood astride a probable trade route along which gold from the west might have passed into the British hinterland and across the Channel to the Continent – probably entering their domain through the Severn estuary. Copper they are more likely to have mined themselves in the south-west, and they almost certainly mined tin – much rarer and therefore widely in demand. There is no direct evidence: almost everywhere all trace of Bronze Age mining has been erased by later workings. But there is the line of cups across the south, with one of gold at either end, and there are finds of distinctive Cornish 'Trevisker' pottery in Kent. There is also – incredibly – a boat.

In a world of unmetalled tracks and animal-drawn carts, overland transport of commodities in bulk was hardly economic. Until the railway age, in fact, goods were moved by preference on water. Bronze Age metals were transported along the coast and navigable rivers. In 1992, towards the end of a long but fairly routine rescue dig in Dover, Keith Parfitt spotted a group of substantial timbers at the bottom of a contractor's trench. They were 20 feet down in the waterlogged levels and the preservation was superb. Climbing down into the

Below: A Bronze Age boat, superbly preserved, emerges from the sludge at the bottom of a contractor's trench in Dover.

trench and beginning to clean back the mud, archaeologists soon revealed the form of a boat. It was over 6 feet wide and formed of two flat base-planks with a hollowed-out quarter tree-trunk on either side. These four main timbers were sewn together with twisted withies. This construction technique was known elsewhere, so there could be no doubt: the boat was Bronze Age. Extra time was negotiated with the developers, and over the following three weeks a 30-foot length of boat – perhaps two-thirds of the total – was cleaned, recorded and lifted for conservation, analysis and eventual public display. The port of Dover, it seems, goes right back to the Bronze Age, and it is a fair guess that tin and copper were among the commodities carried in the earliest boats that used it.

The gold cup Cliff Bradshaw found on the edge of the mound at Ringlemere has revealed part of a lost world. Because the mound was big and the cup special, we can guess that the person buried there was important. Because there are other mounds of the same period, also rich in treasure, we can fit Cliff's discovery into a pattern and begin to reconstruct the shadowy world of the person whose monument it was. We can guess that he belonged to the Wessex 'network' – an aristocracy of Early Bronze Age chieftains and high priests who grew rich on tribute, war booty and the trade in metals. And we can picture him as a warrior who wore his battle gear proudly, boasted of martial achievements and revelled in the drunken feast.

Several gold cups were found in the shaft-graves excavated by Heinrich Schliemann at Mycenae in the late nineteenth century. Schliemann was searching for Homer's heroes. When he saw the riches in the graves he claimed to have found them. In a sense he had. *The Iliad* and *The Odyssey*, though only written down at a much later date, contain traditional accounts of legends passed on over many centuries by oral epic poets. The legends have no certain dates. They are things that happened 'in the olden days'. Many of the objects found in the shaft-graves at Mycenae bear comparison with ones described in the poems. Schliemann found golden cups, and Homer does indeed depict a world where carousing heroes quaff wine from golden cups. The Mycenaean shaft-graves and the Wessex round-barrows were broadly contemporary and, though they cannot compare in wealth, they share common elements of a Europe-wide barbarian warrior culture. So it is a fair guess that Agamemnon would have known what to do with Cliff's cup.

3 Treasure Hoards of the Druids

Treasure Hoards of the Druids

Leicestershire probably has more fieldwalkers than any other county. Fieldwalkers are a funny breed. The director of one top university archaeology department – who had best remain nameless – once remarked, 'Fieldwalking has always struck me as a rather unappealing activity.' It certainly takes commitment to spend hours walking slowly across ploughed fields staring at the ground, looking for that most unattractive of archaeological artefacts: the tiny abraded potsherd. The idea is to record the find-spots, plot them on a map, and thus locate buried archaeological sites according to where there are concentrations of material amid the general background scatter. Actually it can be great fun if you have the right temperament. You work as part of a small team, out in the open air, in contact with the land and the past, and there is a camaraderie among fieldwalkers – lots of banter and laughs over flasks of coffee during breaks beneath windswept hedgerows.

Ken and Hazel Wallace, both retired teachers, are the right sort. They have been fieldwalking for 26 years, ever since long-serving Leicestershire archaeologist Peter Liddle first set up a pioneering community-based fieldwalking programme for the county. Ken is archaeol-

Above: Ken Wallace with some of his finds.

ogical 'warden' for his parish, the leader of a small team of local volunteers, with a hard core of five regulars but up to eight or nine turning out on a good day. One part of the job is to monitor what is going on in the parish from an archaeological standpoint – to look down contractors' holes in the road, check out new building developments, or conduct more formal 'watching briefs' if someone is digging where there might be buried remains. The other part is fieldwalking: regular surveys of cultivated land to see what the latest ploughing has turned up.

It was autumn 2000. Ken had gone over to help out in the neighbouring parish where a new warden had launched her own group. Work had just started investigating a new field about which little was known. They followed the usual Leicestershire procedure of 'traverse and stint'. The field was divided into 10-metre (32-foot) strips which were measured out and marked with canes. Each member of the group then walked a 20-metre (65-foot) length of their strip, collecting artefacts and 'ecofacts' (like bone fragments) on the way. All finds were then bagged and labelled before the next 'traverse' – and so on, slowly across the field. What soon became clear in this particular field was that there was more Iron Age pot than the usual 'background noise', and quite a lot of bone along with it. Ken's long experience told him there was something going on. The field quickly became a priority. More material was recovered in subsequent days. When the fieldwalkers sat down over a glass of wine to identify the finds and plot the distributions, it was clear there was a major Iron Age concentration. Ken became obsessed and went back on his own ten days later; and this time, searching intensively in the Iron Age 'hotspot', he found broken bits of coin and bone on the surface.

Fieldwalkers' eyes are 5-foot off the ground and they rarely see coins and other metal objects, especially when these have been smashed up by ploughing. Ken only found the coins because he was looking closely in one place. To carry on looking like this would distort the results: the more you search, the more you find, but this leaves other areas under-represented when results are plotted. The right tool for this job – a coin hunt – was, of course, a metal-detector. He contacted the farmer who owned the field and got the necessary permission. As soon as he started detecting, there were readings all over the place, and the coins started coming – they seemed to be everywhere across a sizeable chunk of the field. The coins Ken took home at the end of the first day were still covered in clay and had stuck together in a muddy lump. He showed them to Hazel. 'I looked at him and asked if they were Celtic,' she recalls. 'When he told me they were, I couldn't believe it. There were so many. I knew that you never got more than one or two.' In fact, it was the beginning of what was to turn into one of the greatest hauls of Late Iron Age coins ever discovered in British archaeological history. Within a few days, Ken had detected about two hundred, and the archaeological authorities were alerted.

There was now a major problem. The weather was breaking and this made further work on the sticky clay of the field impossible. The coins were glued inside great lumps of the stuff, and Ken found himself trampling crops that were just starting to show as he wrestled for up to a quarter of an hour to recover a single object. Work was stopped for the winter, which meant leaving a highly visible site close to the road vulnerable to destructive raids by nighthawks – so it was vital to keep the discovery secret. The following year work was delayed further by bad weather, the ripening of the crops and then the foot-and-mouth disaster. Not until the autumn could serious work resume. However, the secret had been kept – even the fieldwalkers' own children had not been told about the site. This was just as well. The field, which had already yielded Iron Age coins in unprecedented hundreds, was soon to reveal that it actually contained thousands.

Early British Coins

Who had made the coins? What were they used for? Why were they in the field in such huge numbers? Questions crowd in on a site like this. Coins were first used in Britain shortly before 150 BC. The earliest ones, known as 'Gallo-Belgic' types, are identical to those found on the Continent, and for a long time it was believed they were minted there and came to Britain through trade, payments to mercenaries and gift exchange among the élite. Now experts are not so sure and think the Gallo-Belgics may well have been minted in Britain. Either way, they were not coins in our sense. We shop using large numbers of metallic discs which have token values but are intrinsically almost worthless. Modern currencies work as a method of exchange because people have confidence in them as *symbols* of value. But in 50 BC you could not have bought a cabbage and chicken in the local market with your Gallo-Belgic coins – because they were made of gold and there was no change. Coins of high intrinsic value – gold staters – dominated Celtic currencies, and base-metal coins may never have been

Above and left: Front and back of a Gallo-Belgic A gold stater.

issued in sufficient quantity to replace barter in local markets. 'We should rid our minds of preconceptions and think of Celtic coins not as money but as round metal objects of uncertain use,' says British Museum expert Jonathan Williams. 'Overall they were of too high value to be used as cash. They may have been for very big purchases – a shipment of minerals, say, or wine – but equally they may have been a way for the élite to store wealth, or make political statements about their power, or present offerings to the gods. Quite probably it was all of these – but not cash in the modern sense.'

Round about 70 BC, a new series of 'British derivative' coins began to appear – types exclusive to Britain. Many issues were splendid examples of Celtic art, with its delight in curvilinear shapes, stylized representations of the natural world and weaving together of intricate patterns. The earliest Celtic coins had been modelled on gold staters issued by Philip of Macedon (father of Alexander the Great) in the

Above: An earthenware jar spills out coins found at Stonea Grange in Cambridgeshire.

late fourth century BC. Celtic mercenaries had returned home from the East with bags of Macedonian gold staters depicting Apollo in laurel-wreath crown on the front (the obverse) and a two-horse chariot above the name of the king on the back (the reverse). As Celtic artists took over these designs they transformed them, the divine head becoming a kaleidoscopic swirl of lines, pellets, geometric shapes and laurel leaves, the chariot turning into a highly stylized prancing horse.

The technical side of production was also very skilled. Blanks were made from molten metal cast in clay moulds, the bullion weight of each precisely controlled, and these were then hammered flat to form 'flans'. For most coins – which had images on both sides – there were two dies, a lower one for the obverse image, which was slightly concave to hold the flan in place, and an upper one for the reverse, which was convex and placed over the top. The coin was 'struck' when a single hammer blow impressed the images on the dies into the soft metal of the flan. The equipment required was simple enough, but the skills involved in the whole process – mining, smelting, casting, die-cutting – were formidable. The craftsmen doubtless guarded the 'mysteries' of their trade and were revered as 'magicians'. The patrons who commanded their services were men of power and ambition – men with political agendas and the bullion to back them.

This is soon clear on the coins themselves. Around 30 or 20 BC short, abbreviated inscriptions begin to appear – the name of a ruler, his lineage, his capital, sometimes a claim to royal status. Archaeologically this is a bombshell. It is the first British writing – the first time a British person from the past communicates with us in words. Because writing is new, he uses the Latin script of the Romans, but only occasionally does he borrow foreign words; usually he gives Celtic names. The study of these coin inscriptions and the distribution of different types makes it possible to sketch out possible tribal territories and their political histories. The succession of names, the appearance of one ruler and then another, and a spread of coins in one period and a contraction in the next seem to reflect the rise and fall of rival political authorities.

The Leicestershire Find

What of Ken's coins from a field in Leicestershire? What do we know about this area in the Late Iron Age? From later Roman evidence we gather that the name of the local tribe was 'Corieltauvi',

Below: One side of a Corieltauvian coin found by Ken Wallace, showing an inscription typical of Late Iron Age coins.

and when we try to map out the territory from the distribution of tribal coinage we find them in control of most of the East Midlands and the whole of Lincolnshire. Their early coins, in the later first century BC, were decorated with distinctive adaptations of Celtic or Roman motifs – an arrangement of crescent shapes to represent a horse on gold staters, a realistic and finely engraved boar on silver coins. The early issues were uninscribed, but from the beginning of the first century AD we have a series of abbreviated names: *VEP, AVN AST* or *AVN COST, EVP*

Coins and Politics

The Celtic Coin Index at Oxford has records of many thousands of Iron Age coin finds from Britain and, thanks largely to metal-detecting, hundreds more are being added each year. For example, in 1970 approximately 1,150 coins from the Iceni tribe of Norfolk were recorded; 25 years later, the total was around 13,000, most of these metal-detected in plough-soil. The accumulation of similar metal-detected finds across Britain has resulted in a knowledge explosion: experts now have a much bigger, more representative sample to study, and many previously unknown types of coin have come to light. The outlines of a political history for Britain between *c* 100 BC and AD 50 are now emerging, with the names on later coins sometimes tying in with those recorded in Roman texts.

RASV or *ESVP RASV*, and *VEP CORF*. This is the body of evidence to which Ken's find must now be added. The 3,000 or so coins from a single field is the largest collection ever recovered by archaeologists from one site. They date from the 50 years prior to the Roman Conquest and, as

Above: Front and back of a gold stater of Cunobelinus (CVN), Shakespeare's Cymbeline, king of the Catuvellaunian kingdom, whose main base and mint was at Camulodunum (Colchester), hence the mint mark (CAMV) on his coins.

analysis proceeds, these coins are likely to transform the hazy history of the Corieltauvi. 'We went to a Celtic coin conference in Oxford in December 2001,' recalls Hazel. 'All the experts were there. But English Heritage had said we had to keep the site secret – for fear of nighthawks plundering it before it could be properly investigated. So we pretended we were just interested amateurs. But listening to them, it dawned on us how few coins they knew about. They were talking about dozens and we knew of thousands. It became clear to us just how big our discovery was.' Jonathan Williams, studying the new coins at the British Museum, agrees. 'The sheer quantity gives you a sense of the size of the coinage and how fragmentary our knowledge of it is. The temptation is always to assume that what we've already got is representative of the rest. This is not always true. New finds can defeat our expectations. These certainly do. We've got new types. We've got a whole sweep of silver coins from one place. We can see what's fresher (equals later), what's more worn (equals earlier), and that gives us a relative chronology.'

The value of new knowledge about the Late Iron Age is especially great in the East Midlands. The Corieltauvi are a relatively obscure tribe. Some specialists think in terms of a 'core/periphery model'. In this view, Late Iron Age Britain is divided into three zones. The outer one comprises the highland areas of the north and west – northern England, Wales, and Devon and Cornwall – where coins were never made. The middle zone is the 'peripheral' one, comprising a curving band of territory stretching from northern East Anglia through the Midlands and down into Gloucestershire, Avon, Wiltshire and Dorset. This area, which includes Leicestershire, learns the coin habit, but picks it up second-hand from more developed regions in the south-east. The latter forms the 'core' zone, a group of tribal states in direct contact with the Gauls and Romans across the Channel. Here were the two most powerful Late Iron Age kingdoms: that of the Catuvellauni north of the Thames in Hertfordshire and Essex; and that of the Atrebates south of the river, in Berkshire and Hampshire. The south-east was the real powerhouse of Late Iron Age Britain, and it is here that we can discover where new developments in a fast-changing world were leading.

By coincidence, just as Ken was finding his field of coins in Leicestershire, someone else, out detecting on the Hampshire Downs near Winchester, was making an equally spectacular discovery in the heartlands of the Atrebatic 'Southern Kingdom'.

The Hampshire Find

The first indications of a major find had come in September 2000. Sally Worrell, then finds liaison officer for Hampshire, had received a call from Kevan Halls. She knew him to be an experienced and busy metal-detectorist. He owned five machines and, while his wife minded their florist's shop, he was often out several times a week. He had previously trawled the field where he was now working two or three times, but without much success. Then, moving to a new area, he had found an astonishing treasure: first a gold brooch with a fine gold chain still attached, and, a few minutes later, a second brooch, the twin of the first. He had taken the finds home and placed them on the kitchen table for his wife to see. She had come home, started cooking and noticed nothing until midway through eating dinner. 'She practically fell off her chair when she saw them,' recalls Kevan. When he broke the news on the phone to Sally Worrell, she persuaded him to bring the brooches into the Winchester Museum straight away. Kevan had guessed they were Roman. Sally was not sure, and so the brooches were taken to the British Museum, where J.D. Hill identified them as Late Iron Age and exceptionally rare.

J.D. – as he is known to his colleagues – had no trouble with the identification because the form of the brooches was familiar: they were 'safety pin' brooches of a type known by the German name *Knotenfibeln*, and they dated to *c*70–30 BC. Examples were known from cemeteries on both sides of the Channel, and they often occurred in pairs because the Late Iron Age practice was to pin a cloak together with two brooches and a chain. However, the great majority of such objects were bronze. A mere dozen or so of those that had been found were gold.

But there was more to come. Kevan continued detecting in the field that autumn, Sally's phone kept ringing, and the final haul was two gold jewellery sets, each one comprising a necklace torc, two brooches and a chain (though only one chain was found), and a bracelet. One necklace torc was notably bigger than the other, as if these two sets of personal ornaments had been a matching pair for a man and a woman. Not only was so much gold in one place exceptional – with a current market value of £350,000 – but the use of gold, its quality and the style of the artefacts could not be fitted into any simple Late Iron Age pattern. There was a far from straightforward story here about wealth and power and contacts in the Southern Kingdom. For one thing, gold was rarely used except for coins. For another, this gold was above 90 per cent pure. Analysis by 'X-ray fluorescence spectrometry' of small, cleaned surfaces on the artefacts revealed lower proportions of copper and silver than is ever found in Celtic coins of the period. Only the Romans produced gold as good as this. Then there were the goldworking techniques. Both necklace torcs were fastened by clasps, the construction and decoration of which were unknown to Celtic craftsmen. When magnified under a 'scanning electron microscope', the clasp on the smaller torc revealed that it was a tube of gold on to which decoration in the form of 'granulation' (gold globules) and 'filigree' (gold wire) had been fixed by a technique called 'diffusion soldering'. Instead of using another metal with a lower melting point as solder, the diffusion method used a mixture of glue and copper compound which alloyed with the gold to produce an invisible bond. Again, only the Romans knew how to do this. Finally, there was the style and finesse of the objects. Iron Age torcs were usually rigid when worn, but the two necklaces and the chain in the Winchester hoard were flexible. J.D. Hill remembers getting a strange call from Sally Worrell. 'She said she had a snake-like gold torc. It was difficult to imagine. But she was right. It flows.' It flows because it is formed of loop-in-loop chains made by threading and bending wire rings through each other – a common enough technique in the Roman Empire, but unknown in Celtic Europe.

Despite the 'Romanized' techniques used to manufacture the Winchester treasures, torcs were essentially Celtic, and not Roman artifacts. Made of precious or base metal, often elaborately worked and decorated, they comprised a hoop flexible enough to be got on and off the neck, and two opposing terminals. The finest known is the great gold torc from Snettisham in Norfolk. 'The hoop of this torc,' explains Ian Longworth of the British Museum's prehistory department, 'is made of

Below: The Winchester hoard, two matching sets of Late Iron Age gold jewellery of the highest quality.

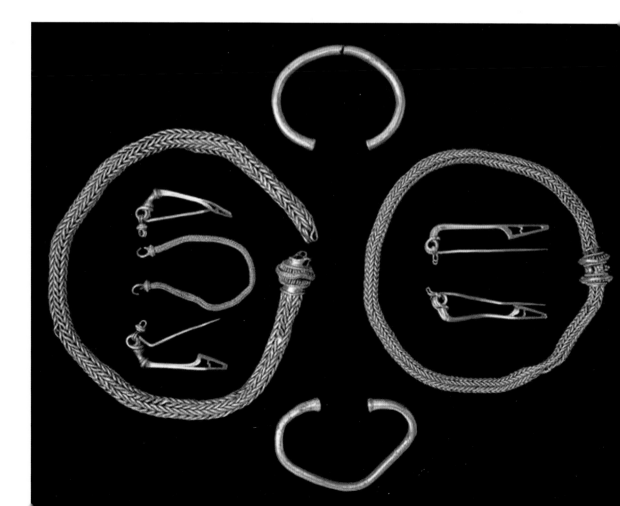

The Torc – Status Symbol of the Celtic Warrior

Torcs are depicted in sculpture and referred to in literature. 'Very terrifying, too, were the appearance and gestures of the naked warriors in front, all in the prime of life and finely built men, and all in the leading companies richly adorned with gold torcs and armlets'

wrote the Greek historian Polybius, describing the Celtic battle-array at the battle of Telamon in 225 BC. Almost 300 years later, according to another writer of Roman history, Greek senator Dio Cassius, Boudicca was 'very tall and grim, her gaze penetrating, her voice harsh, and she grew her long auburn hair down to her hips, and wore a large gold torc and a huge patterned cloak with a thick plaid fastened over it'. Dio may not, in fact, be a reliable source for Boudicca's actual appearance, but he knew how a Celtic warrior-queen ought to look. For him and other classical writers, torcs were well-known symbols of an exotic barbarian warrior-culture.

Above: An artist's reconstruction showing the jewellery found in the Winchester hoard, as it might have been worn by a Celtic couple.

eight ropes of wire twisted together, each rope made up of eight wires similarly twisted. The massive hollow terminal rings carry lobes modelled in relief, and these are coupled with complex tendrils filled with cross-hatched hurdle pattern.' The great torc forms part of the richest hoard of Iron Age treasure ever found: dozens of gold, electrum, silver and bronze torcs in 12 separate deposits scattered across an area of some 3 acres. But there have also been many isolated finds and occasional small groups elsewhere.

The curious thing about the Winchester hoard is that you have Celtic artefacts crafted from Roman gold, using Roman techniques, in a Roman style. What does it mean? Stuart Needham, another of the British Museum's prehistory specialists, was quoted in the local press arguing that it symbolized the cultural fusion going on in a changing world:

The objects show a level of technology that has been brought in from the classical world. They [the British Celts] were clearly in some modes of life extremely sophisticated. They did not have highly developed political structures, but they did have refined ideas of social ranking. The exceptional thing is that these so-called 'barbarians' not only copied Hellenistic styles, but writ them large. They not only created big thick ropes of chain in their traditional style, but also adapted them with a great deal of imagination and finesse. The couple who wore this jewellery would have been part of the élite. They were making a definite statement by portraying not only their wealth, as shown in the gold, but also their connections with a wider world through its sophisticated style.

Below: The Dying Gaul. A Greek sculpture reputed to have belonged to Julius Caesar, which depicts a Celtic warrior wearing a torc.

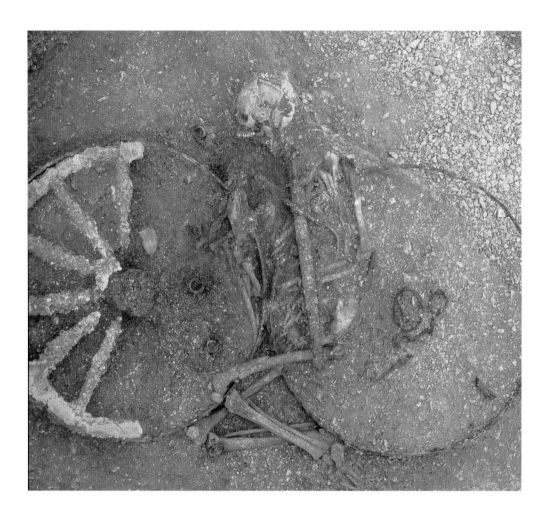

Above: A rich warrior burial from Wetwang in eastern Yorkshire, where body and grave-goods overlie the remains of a dismantled chariot.

The mix of Celtic and Roman seems to run through everything from this period. Rich burials came back into fashion in the Late Iron Age after not being seen for a long period. Among the grave-goods, a new Roman fashion is often much in evidence. We sometimes find decorated bronze flagons or engraved silver drinking-cups from southern Italy; or fine ceramic tablewares from northern Italy or Gaul – 'red ware' (*terra rubra*), 'black ware' (*terra nigra*) or Arretine ware with its glossy orange surface. Also included might be a collection of amphorae, the large storage vessels in which Romans transported such Mediterranean luxuries as wine, olive oil and the pungent fish-sauce they used to spice up bland food. Alongside these foreign luxuries, meanwhile, was the paraphernalia of Celtic warrior culture. We find it sometimes in the grave alongside the Roman dining sets, sometimes ritually deposited in some remote and holy spot in the ancient wilderness. Much of it is war-gear: decorated bronze scabbards and shield-facings, iron swords and spearheads, chariot fittings and bits of horse harness, and of course the torcs, armlets and other personal ornaments favoured by warriors. In eastern Yorkshire – though only here – the richest of these were interred with the remains of their chariots, several of which have been excavated in an Iron Age cemetery near the village of Wetwang. Dark stains reveal the position of rotted woodwork – the wheels, the axle, the central pole. Rusted lumps of iron turn out to be horse-bits, linchpins or the remains of metal tyres, and corroded rings of enamelled bronze are the remains of 'terrets' attached to the yoke through which the reins once passed. These were vehicles of a kind seen by Caesar on the battlefields of ancient Britain, as he later recalled:

> In chariot fighting, the Britons begin by driving all over the field hurling javelins, and generally the terror inspired by the horses and the noise of the wheels are sufficient to throw their opponents' ranks into disorder. Then ... they jump down from the chariots and engage on foot, while their charioteers retire a short distance from the battle and place the chariots in such a position that their masters, if hard pressed by numbers, have an easy means of retreat to their own lines. Thus they combine the mobility of cavalry with the staying power of infantry. And by daily training and practice, they attain such proficiency that even on a steep incline they are able to control the horses at full gallop, and to check and turn them in a moment. They can run along the chariot pole, stand on the yoke, and get back into the chariot as quick as lightning.

As well as war-gear, there were also iron firedogs for the feast, bronze-plated buckets for beer or mead, and mirrors of highly polished metal. All this élite metalwork was decorated by Celtic artists working in the La Tène tradition. Britain, indeed, as the last part of the Celtic world to remain beyond Roman control, produced the final and finest flowering of

La Tène art. Shields, scabbards, buckets, mirrors, torcs and brooches were covered in swirling designs of curves, circles and scrolls, sometimes incised, sometimes embossed, often enhanced with inlays of red enamel. Occasionally, in the twists and turns, the stylized heads of animals appear, perhaps glaring at one another on either end of an open hoop. But mainly La Tène is an abstract art where the rounded shapes of nature have lost all recognizable form and been reduced to a complex play of lines. The result is decoration of extraordinary beauty. Objects such as the Battersea Shield and the Desborough Mirror in the British Museum collection are among the world's artistic masterpieces. These were the artefacts and decorative designs of the Late Iron Age aristocracy. 'When their services are required in some war that has broken out,' reports Caesar in his description of Celtic society, 'the war-chiefs all take the field, surrounded by their servants and retainers, of whom each chief has a greater or smaller number according to his birth and fortune. The possession of such a following is the only criterion of position and power that they recognize.'

Left: The Battersea Shield, a masterpiece of La Tène art.

Trade in the Late Iron Age

It was into an essentially Homeric world of warriors, battle-gear and barbarian art that Mediterranean luxuries were now beginning to intrude. Kevan Halls' torcs, with their mix of Celtic type and Roman technique, symbolize the intrusion. Was it just a matter of changing fashion, an expanding market and local merchants with some entrepreneurial flair? The Greek geographer Strabo, writing at this time, certainly makes it sound so. He tells us that the Britons were exporting 'corn, cattle, gold, silver and iron' along with 'hides, slaves and hunting dogs'. But he gives the impression that they got little in return – 'ivory bracelets and necklaces, amber and glassware, and similar petty trifles' – as if the simple natives were being swindled by canny foreign traders. The archaeology tells a different story: top-ranking

Britons were receiving goods of real value, and there is no good reason for thinking that they were caught up in a system of 'unequal exchange'. Indeed, to get to the heart of what was going on, we need to shed most of our modern ideas about how valuable goods get moved around. In our world – a capitalist global economy – trade is dominated by big corporations buying and selling to make a profit. The great powers fight wars mainly for commercial advantage – for raw materials, protected markets and opportunities to invest capital. They are after the big-money commodities – slaves and sugar in the eighteenth-century West Indies, say, South African gold or Turkish railway contracts a hundred years ago, or Middle Eastern oil today. The problem is that none of this modern experience is remotely useful in understanding Late Iron Age Britain. The world then worked in completely different ways.

Above: Kevan Halls discusses his finds with series presenter Miranda Krestovnikoff.

Most production was subsistence level and very local. The majority of people – perhaps as many as nine in ten – were peasants who satisfied their daily needs from their own farms or by swapping things with community craftsmen. Hundreds of Iron Age farmsteads have been excavated. One of the first was Little Woodbury in Wiltshire. A circular ditch enclosed some 4 acres, and within were the remains of round-houses built of timber, wattle-and-daub and thatch, underground pits for storing seed corn, raised granaries for food corn, drying racks for the winter fodder, and an irregular 'working hollow' where farmyard and domestic chores were carried out. The material culture at sites like this is usually pretty basic: sherds of hand-thrown local pottery, stone loom-weights and bone weaving equipment, bits of ironwork from agricultural tools – the stuff essential for everyday life on a mixed subsistence farm in prehistoric Britain. The goods that were traded long distances, by contrast, were of two kinds: bulk commodities for big institutional consumers such as the Roman government or its army; and specialized or luxury items for an élite clientele. Strabo's list of British exports fits in well: corn, cattle, hides and iron perhaps to supply the Roman army on the Rhine; gold and silver for the imperial mints; and slaves and hunting dogs for the villa aristocracy.

But we should not think of even élite goods as trade commodities in our sense. No doubt there was some regular trade – and swindling – carried on by merchants who were in it for profit. But they were not operating in a 'free market'. The ancient economy was 'embedded' in the social structure: commerce was subordinate to political authority. Route-ways, ports and markets were controlled. You had to get permission to buy, move and sell goods, and the rights to do these things were privileges which powerful men could bestow on those they favoured as a way of enhancing their power. Hengistbury Head near Christchurch on the south coast – within the territory of our putative Southern Kingdom – must have been part of just such a controlled economy in the early first century BC. Wine, figs and glassware are among the Mediterranean imports in evidence there. Whoever controlled the port enjoyed exclusive access to the luxury goods it handled, and this was a source of patronage and power. Anthropologists talk of 'primitive valuables' – special goods that are valued for their rarity, exoticism, fine craftsmanship or expensive materials – the possession and distribution of which confer status and rank. Remember Caesar's description of the Celtic noble's retinue – where the size of each war-chief's following reflected his birth and fortune, and this was the measure of his eminence. When a great lord gave presents to his retainers – especially of items otherwise unobtainable – he cemented their allegiance and built up his power. Wine, gold and battle-gear made Iron Age armies.

Imperial Favours

Luxury goods were not only traded; they were also given. But if they could be the gifts of kings to loyal followers, they could also be the gifts of emperors to loyal kings. Rarely has anything so rich as Kevan Halls' Winchester hoard come to light, and though Roman or Roman-trained artisans might have made the objects for a Celtic patron, it seems more likely that they were gifts from Caesar – chips of gold in the diplomatic poker game of the first century BC. That there were contacts between Britain and Rome at the highest level is beyond question. Between Caesar's expeditions in 55 and 54 BC and the Claudian invasion of AD 43, we hear of several high-ranking British nobles who sought refuge on the Continent. They often lobbied for Roman military support to restore them to power; sometimes they got it, sometimes not. Caesar helped Mandubracius to take the throne of the Trinovantes tribe in 54 BC, but his successor Augustus, while welcoming Dubnovellaunus and perhaps one Tincomarus 'as suppliants' – and no doubt keeping them on hand against a time when they might be useful – never went ahead with a threatened invasion of Britain. The mad emperor Caligula, on the other hand, tried and failed: in AD 40 his grand invasion never got off the beaches – probably because the army mutinied – and he tried to cover up the fiasco by presenting another British exile, the prince Adminius, as evidence of a non-existent victory. Three years later, according to Dio Cassius, 'a certain Berikos, who had been driven out of the island as a result of civil war, persuaded Claudius to send a force there'; this must be the ruler whose name – in the Latinate form 'Verica' – appears on British coins of the Southern Kingdom in the early first century AD.

Our written sources are sparse. We usually hear about British exiles only in the context of war, real or threatened. The diplomacy linking Britain and Rome was probably elaborate, with ambassadors, military attachés, the payment of subsidies (today's 'aid packages'), 'official visits' (including gift exchange), technical assistance (such as Roman die-cutters for making coins) and, not least perhaps, a Roman education for favoured royal princes, followed by a stint as an 'officer cadet' in the Roman imperial army. John Manley and John Creighton, two specialists on the Late Iron Age, see much evidence for full-blown 'client-kingdoms' in southern Britain in the hundred years before the Roman Conquest. Empires have always promoted puppet rulers. For the Romans, it was a standard part of the diplomatic armoury. Here is the Roman biographer Suetonius describing how it worked under Augustus:

> Except in a few instances, he restored the kingdoms of which he had gained possession by the right of conquest to those from whom he had taken them or joined them with other foreign nations. He also united the kings with whom he was in alliance by mutual ties, and was very ready to propose or favour intermarriages or friendships among them. He never failed to treat them all with consideration as integral parts of the empire, regularly appointing a guardian for such as were too young to rule or whose minds were affected, until they grew up or recovered; and he brought up the children of many of them and educated them with his own.

The idea was to create buffer states around the edge of the empire: local rulers retained formal independence but had the advantage of Roman support against their enemies; the Romans got frontier security at minimal cost.

Fishbourne in Sussex – another site within the Southern Kingdom – is famous for having a Roman palace from the late first century AD. Fit for a king, the best guess is that it was indeed a king, or at least one of his immediate descendants, who owned it. We even know the name: Tiberius Claudius Togidubnus was, according to an inscription dug up in 1723 at Chichester a mile or so from the palace, 'Great King of the Britons'; and, according to Tacitus, he 'maintained his unswerving loyalty right down to our own times – an example of the long-established Roman custom of employing even kings to make others slaves'. So, early in the Roman period Chichester was the capital of a British client-kingdom, with the royal palace just outside at Fishbourne. What was the palace earlier, before the Conquest? New excavations are revising old ideas. A Conquest-period army base has long been suspected, but John Manley's team now also suspect that a metalled road, military-style buildings and large hauls of Roman pottery all date to much earlier in the first century AD. Fishbourne's 'Roman' archaeology, in other words, seems to start well *before* AD 43. The place was already in some sense 'Roman' when the legions arrived. Verica, the last king of the Southern Kingdom before the Conquest, the ruler whose flight from Britain was the pretext for war, was probably a client-king of Rome all along. No surprise, then, that his coins appear to announce a Roman allegiance: there are naturalistic vine leaves and Roman horsemen; the Latin *REX* is used for the royal title; and, perhaps imitating the style of Verica's imperial patrons, the Roman emperors, we have the formula *COM.F*, 'son of Commius', to assert his lineage and legitimacy.

Royal Rivalries

Verica left Britain because his kingdom was under attack from the north. The Catuvellaunian kingdom had been expanding for half a century. The details are obscure – and will probably never be settled – but the general impression from coin evidence is of an emerging Celtic superpower, absorbing its neighbours one after the other, doubtless through some mixture of intrigue, alliance, threats and war. The death of the old king, Cunobelinus – Shakespeare's Cymbeline – seems to have placed control of the

Catuvellauni in the hands of two ambitious young princes, Caratacus and Togodumnus, and brought to a crisis the growing tension with the Southern Kingdom. The core zone of Late Iron Age Britain was highly unstable. All evidence points in one direction: towards the formation of royal states through the amalgamation

Above: The Iron Age and Romano-British village of Chysauster, Cornwall. Each enclosure, built of dry-stone walling, contained a small open courtyard and a series of rooms opening onto it – home presumably to a family unit.

– by agreement or by force – of smaller tribal units. Centuries before, in the Early Iron Age, much of the landscape had been dominated by small hill-forts commanding a territory only a few miles broad. There were no great burial mounds, no coins, no claims to royal status. It was a world of local chieftains, personal retinues and a dependent peasantry known face-to-face. By the Late Iron Age, most of the hill-forts had been abandoned, even some of the biggest, and the settlements that dominated the south-eastern half of the island were great sprawling *oppida*, their dykes and ramparts enclosing huge areas where cattle could be corralled, chariots parked and large royal households maintained. The names of these places are sometimes inscribed on the coins – *VER* for Verulamium (St Albans), *CAMU* for Camulodunum (Colchester) and *CALL* for Calleva (Silchester). The mint debris is often there, too, in the form of fragments of the clay moulds used for making metal blanks. Here, in a sense, is written testimony to the state-building ambition of Britain's first kings. And sometimes the short run of a name on coins – like the passing reference to an exile in the ancient texts – is testimony also to the fragility of their power. States and dynasties struggled for life. The rival war-bands played a lethal game. The losers perished or fled. The victors, insecure and threatened, attacked again lest they be attacked, trapped in a permanent war that could logically end only when all possible rivals had been vanquished.

In Gosbecks Park at Camulodunum, local archaeologist Philip Crummy thinks he has located the residence of King Cunobelinus, and in excavations at nearby Stanway the burial ground of the Catuvellaunian dynasty. But what about the wearers of the Winchester jewellery? Where were they from? Rarely has anything so rich been found in Late Iron Age Britain. The owners must have been of royal rank. So where were their *oppidum*, their royal kraal and their great burial mounds?

There is no doubt that the jewellery *was* worn. Microscopic analysis revealed the tell-tale wear patterns on some of the metal. The expert official report was unequivocal:

All four brooches show little obvious wear on their pins, which is unusual given the soft nature of the gold. This contrasts with the very noticeable wear on their collared links where they were attached to their chains and on the wire of the surviving brooch chain. This wear is consistent with the pull that would be exerted by the weight of clothing, and also indicates that the brooches were worn with their spring end uppermost. The lack of wear on the pins might suggest they were not often unfastened. Perhaps the cloak was taken off over the wearer's head without unpinning the brooches. Alternatively, could the lack of wear on the pins suggest the wearers did not dress themselves but had other people pinning and unpinning the brooches for them?

So these objects were not simply 'primitive valuables' to be hoarded as symbols of wealth. They were actually used. They were worn, and often. So, soon after Kevan's first discoveries in the field, the hunt was on for an 'archaeological context' in which to place the objects and their owners.

In Search of a Palace

As it happens, a few miles from where the Winchester hoard was found, an Iron Age settlement was excavated in the 1960s. By the late first century BC it had become a big place, the main enclosure extending across 6 acres of a gentle downland slope. There was a ditch around the perimeter, four or five entrances, and a series of trackways, some cobbled, leading up to the enclosure through the surrounding fields. Inside were the pits and post holes of a typical Iron Age farm. It is easy to imagine the little collection of round-houses, raised granaries and drying racks on the hill, the corn growing in small square fields immediately round about, animals being moved along the cobbled tracks towards the pasture beyond, and the limits of the farm visible as a stand of woodland in the distance. Was this a nobleman's residence? Certainly it was above average. In one of the earliest layers, archaeologists discovered a linchpin of the kind used to attach the wheel of a chariot to its axle. Like many other examples – and war-gear generally – it was highly decorated. Though made of iron, it had bronze terminals with embossed designs, one showing a 'figure 2' motif, the other a 'triskelion' in the style of the Isle of Man motif. If the chariot from which the object fell – it was found on a trackway – belonged to the owner of the farm, then he was indeed a nobleman.

One linchpin does not make a noble residence, of course. An adjacent warrior burial is quite a different matter, however. The site is unusual for the Iron Age in having its own cemetery. Two rectangular enclosures were attached to the north side of the main enclosure, and each of these contained a rich burial. One was of a man of about 40 or 50 years, laid out full length on his back and accompanied by spear, sword and shield. The spear was represented by its iron head and butt end; it had been laid across the body, but apparently snapped in two. The long iron sword lay beside the body, with traces of a wooden sheath beneath it. And the shield, probably a full-length body-shield, must have been laid on top of the deceased, for an elaborate bronze 'butterfly' boss (with splayed

All-terrain Vehicles of the Iron Age

Chariots were hugely expensive. To be battle-worthy they had to be light for speed yet strong for durability, and that meant they had to be expertly constructed from quality timber. Openwork wheels were essential and some, with as many as 12 spokes, must have been masterpieces of the wheelwright's craft. Vehicles were routinely finished with many beautifully decorated metal parts. Two strong, healthy, well-trained ponies were needed to pull them. The driver would have to be highly skilled. Chariots, in short, were the battle-carts of tribal aristocrats. Caesar tells us that in 54 BC his British opponent, Cassivellaunus, the most powerful ruler in south-east Britain, commanded a force of 4,000 chariots. These, it is clear, formed his warrior élite: his infantry – a tribal levy of peasants – he chose to send home to tend the fields.

wings on either side of the central point) was found above the lower vertebrae. There was also a tinned bronze belt-hook – almost certainly a Continental import of the first century BC. Other imports were in evidence elsewhere on the site, such as fine wheel-thrown tablewares of similar date from Gaul. Here was confirmation that 2,000 years ago this was indeed the centre of a minor nobleman's estate.

Nevertheless this warrior was hardly a candidate for ownership of the Winchester jewellery. A retainer, perhaps – quite likely a man known personally to those who *did* own it – but no more than that. Determined to find out more, a small team of archaeologists from the British and Winchester museums went to Kevan's field to look for the buried remains of the site from which the treasures had come. Kevan had been conscientious about plotting his find-spots. Most of the artefacts had come from a small area about 80 feet across on a gentle hill-crest at the top of the field. The exceptions had been moved along the path taken by a plough – the two brooches with chain 400 feet to the south, the smaller necklace torc about 650 feet to the north. All the objects recovered from the plough-soil showed signs of damage, but the small necklace torc in particular looked as if it had been caught up on the end of a plough or harrow and then fallen off when the tractor turned at the edge of the field. Everything pointed towards the small area on the crest.

But there was nothing. No earthworks were visible on the surface, however slight, and no buried features showed on the geophysics. The test pits revealed only ploughing and subsoil. The one bright spot was Kevan's detecting, for it was at this time that the last of the treasures was found. There was only one possible conclusion: whatever sort of site this was, the plough had finally destroyed it, removing all trace of it as it cut down into the subsoil deeper than any Iron Age pits or ditches had ever gone. The battered gold objects, uprooted from their resting place after 2,000 years, were all that remained.

The dig ended in the spring of 2001. The following autumn, half-way across the country in Leicestershire, another team of archaeologists started digging up Ken Wallace's field of coins. Here they were in luck.

A Professional Dig

At first, the Leceistershire field had not looked promising. Trial trenches on the site of geophysics anomalies revealed a Roman settlement of the third and fourth centuries AD, but nothing contemporary with the coins. It was Ken's little flags that saved the day. A victory for old tech. As an experienced fieldwalker, Ken had been meticulous about precise recording of his find-spots, and now, challenging the negative geophysics head-on, he re-plotted the positions and planted his flags to show the archaeologists where to put their trenches. Worried about the vulnerability of such a rich site, English Heritage had coughed up the funds for a professional dig, and Vicki Priest had been put in charge of the Leicester University Archaeological Services team commissioned to do the job. Some of its members were a bit sceptical about the flags. Ken, on the other hand, was a bit sceptical about the heavy machinery. The problem with professional units – units where everything is costed on a commercial basis – is that you have to cut corners. Ideally, you would dig a site like this by hand from the very top: that way you would minimize damage to any finds in the plough-soil, and you could be certain not to 'over-cut' and go into the undisturbed archaeology beneath. With volunteers on a research dig, that would be fine; with paid staff, it is plain uneconomic. Especially now, with archaeology more or less 'privatized' so that units are competing ruthlessly for contracts. Costs are paramount if a unit is to survive in the open market, and sacrifices are made – both with the jobs, pay and conditions of professional diggers, and with the archaeology itself. There are some out-and-out cowboy

Above: An exquisitely crafted ceremonial Roman-cavalry helmet found at Xanten-Wardt in Germany, of the same type as the one found by Ken Wallace.

units. And there are horror stories that get retold in the tea-sheds by old hands 'on the circuit'. This is 'the real world' – which means the world imposed by politicians – within which all professional site directors have to operate. Vicki had no choice but to machine off the plough-soil – even though it was full of Iron Age coins and she could not be sure how deep it would be.

No one on the team had ever seen anything quite like what then appeared. As the machine bucket – a toothless one to give a smooth scrape – pulled back the topsoil, it revealed a surface 'speckled with little green blobs and the odd coin popping out'. Most diggers expect one or two Iron Age coins on a site. Sometimes they get none. Here, laid out before them, were hundreds still *in situ*, some arranged in the shape of the bags that had contained them.

The site was damaged, of course. Ken had already found hundreds of coins that had been disturbed in the plough-soil and now, detecting furiously in the spoil coming off the site in the machine bucket, he found hundreds more. The fieldwalking team joined in detecting the spoil, finding coins so quickly that if a couple of minutes passed without one, they would run the detector over the rivets on their boots to check the batteries were still functioning. But the plough had only sliced away the tops of the features. The bottoms of ditches and pits were still there. Vicki's team found a boundary ditch enclosing the site, with an elaborate entrance, and 13 coin groups in the enclosure. Before the dig ended, the coin total would approach 3,000, and the bulk would have come from the 'primary deposits' – that is, from the pits where they had originally been placed in the Iron Age. Even now, with excavation proceeding, the metal-detector remained a key tool. 'I think we changed the way the professionals work,' muses Ken. 'The unit actually purchased a metal-detector and I gave them lessons in how to use it. They replaced their nails with plastic pegs to avoid creating false readings. We were metal-detecting every teaspoonful of soil, and the professionals realized it had to be done. It was amazing what came out of that area!'

Ken was using his detector routinely to warn the excavators when and where they should expect metal. Late one afternoon he got a signal near the edge of the site, and when he returned the following morning the diggers were already at work there. They had found a silver ear.

Only later would the identity of this curious object be revealed. Patrick Clay, the head of the unit and a veteran of Leicestershire archaeology, was shown it in his office, and he knew immediately what it was. He had dug one up years before in Leicester itself – one of only a handful found in Britain so far. The silver ear was part of a gilded iron parade-helmet of the kind worn by Roman auxiliary cavalry during military tattoos.

The diggers did not know this at the time, but it was clear enough that they were dealing with a complete 'ritual deposit'. The decision was therefore taken to carry out a 'block lift' of helmet, coins and surrounding soil, so that everything could be excavated carefully in the British Museum conservation lab. Some jobs take as long as they take: something as special as this should not be done in the field under a time constraint.

Ancient Celtic Paganism

Without doubt, the field was a religious site. Up to 3,000 gold, silver and base-metal coins had been ritually deposited in pits within an enclosure. This had happened over about half a century immediately prior to the Roman Conquest. Other valuable objects had also been deliberately placed here: the cavalry helmet, Roman brooches, the end of a gold bracelet or necklace, and huge numbers of pig bones. However, there was no evidence for settlement, for domestic occupation, for people going about their ordinary everyday lives. No one had lived here in the Late Iron Age, but they had come here, quite often, and when they came it was for a very special purpose. In Ken's field of coins, we penetrate deeply into the religious mysteries of the ancient Celts.

We know the names of about two hundred Celtic deities, but we know them second-hand. Greek and Roman writers, Roman-period inscriptions and later Irish literature are our main sources. These are no more than scattered written fragments, and the archaeological record is fragmentary too, so we end up with what one scholar has called a 'fertile chaos' – lots of bits of evidence resulting in confusion. Barry Cunliffe, Oxford professor and top Iron Age specialist, nonetheless thinks he can see a pattern:

Left: The head of a Celtic god from Corbridge near Hadrian's Wall. The date is Roman but the style and subject thoroughly Celtic.

It would be unwise to try to structure Celtic religion … rigidly … Yet, among the multiplicity and mobility of titles and powers exhibited by the Celtic gods, it is possible to detect an underlying structure of simple binary oppositions: male/tribe/sky/war against female/place/earth/ fertility. The coupling of the two produces balance, harmony and productivity, and has to be enacted on a regular annual cycle determined by the seasons.

The Celtic 'Death of the Year'

The Celts were a people of farmers and herdsmen, and the seasons, the agricultural cycle and the fertility of land and stock were the primary focus of religion. In late autumn, for instance, with the harvest in and winter approaching, the old year died and there was cold and darkness and fear. The spirits of the dead walked at this time. So Celts celebrated the festival of Samain, when the male tribal god Dagda impregnated the female fertility goddess Morrigan, restoring her youth and vitality, and ensuring the fertility of crops and animals in the year to come. We celebrate it still: it is Hallowe'en.

The sun-worshippers of Stonehenge had given way to the adherents of a pantheon of power gods and earth mothers – but there was still a caste of priests. Their existence in the Early Bronze Age is strongly suspected, yet they remain invisible. By the Late Iron Age, they have come into the light of day: several ancient writers tell us that Celtic priests were called 'druids', and two Celtic languages, Old Irish and Welsh, record this title. The fullest account of them has been left by Caesar, who tells us that they presided over holy rites, ruled on religious matters, acted as judges in both criminal and civil cases, and were the bearers of Celtic traditions. As priests, scholars and magistrates they were, unsurprisingly, part of the élite. Exempt from taxes and military service, supported by levies imposed on a peasant population that Caesar describes as little better than slaves, they were equal in rank to the warrior nobles. And the religion of the druids could be an awesome instrument of social control. 'Any individual or tribe failing to accept their [the druids'] decision,'

Caesar explains, 'is banned from taking part in sacrifice – the heaviest punishment that can be inflicted on a Gaul. Those who are laid under such a ban are regarded as impious criminals. Everyone shuns them and avoids going

Opposite: A fanciful 1815 image of a druid - but the white robes are referred to by a reputable Roman writer.

near or speaking to them, for fear of taking some harm by contact with what is unclean. If they appear as plaintiffs, justice is denied them, and they are excluded from a share in any honour.' The power of ostracism must have made the druids feared. Since, moreover, they were the indispensable intermediaries between gods and men, they wielded also the threat of divine wrath. Some of the gruesome holy rites over which they presided surely chilled the spines of their flocks. Their grip on Celtic society must have been tight.

What was druidic ritual like? You might have answered that question in Roman times by reaching for your encyclopaedia – or calling a slave to fetch it:

> The druids … hold nothing more sacred than mistletoe and the tree on which it grows, provided it is hard-oak. … they do not perform any sacred rites without leaves from these trees … For they believe that anything growing on oak-trees is sent by heaven and is a sign that the tree has been chosen by God himself. Mistletoe, however, is rarely found on hard-oaks, but when it is discovered, it is collected with great respect on the sixth day of the moon. Then, greeting the moon with the phrase that in their own language means 'healing all things', the druids with due religious observance prepare a sacrifice and banquet beneath a tree, and bring two white bulls whose horns are bound for the first time. A priest in a white robe climbs the tree and with a golden sickle cuts the mistletoe, which is caught in a white cloak. Then they sacrifice the victims, praying that God may make his gift propitious for those to whom he has given it. They think that mistletoe given in a drink renders any barren animal fertile and is an antidote for all poisons. (Pliny the Elder, *Natural History*, mid first century AD)

There are elements here common to all ancient religions. The gods are appeased by offerings and worship; they can be manipulated, bribed, brought to act as people wish them to through human actions. The natural world is saturated with their presence, so much so that many ordinary things, as if touched by a god, have magical properties. Ritual and magic are precise sciences: any mistake, any deviation from the rule, might violate a taboo, pollute the worshippers and invoke divine wrath. So a caste of professional priests learned in traditional lore is an essential intermediary. Only its members know, always, what must be done. In another sense, druidism is a very practical religion. It is less concerned with the afterlife than with the immediate problems of life today. The gods' help is sought in ensuring the passage of the seasons, the fruitfulness of the land and the survival of the tribe.

Sacred Groves

Where did sacrifice take place? Did druids build temples? Should we expect a temple inside the enclosure in Ken's field and, if so, what would it look like? Some Celtic ritual sites certainly had temples. They were usually substantial, square, timber buildings – though they could also be circular – sometimes with a surrounding palisade of timber uprights. But many more sites are known which lack any obvious structure, and ancient sources confirm that Celtic deities often resided beneath the open sky in wild natural places. The Roman poet Lucan, in his *Pharsalia*, has left us with a vivid description of a 'sacred grove' in southern Gaul around the middle of the first century BC.

A grove there was untouched by men's hands from ancient times, whose interlacing boughs enclosed a space of darkness and cold shade, and banished the sunlight from above … gods were worshipped there with savage rites, the altars were heaped with hideous offerings, and every tree was sprinkled with human gore. On those boughs … birds feared to perch; in those coverts, wild beasts would not lie down; no wind ever bore down upon that wood, nor thunderbolt hurled from black clouds; the trees, even when they spread their leaves to no breeze, rustled of themselves. Water, also, fell there in abundance from dark springs. The images of the gods grim and rude were uncouth blocks formed of felled tree-trunks. Their mere antiquity and the ghastly hue of the rotten timber struck terror. … Legend also told that often the subterranean hollows quaked and bellowed, that yew trees fell down and rose again, that the glare of conflagrations came from trees that were not on fire, and that serpents twined and glided round their stems. The people never resorted thither to worship at close quarters, but left the place to the gods. For, when the sun is in mid-heaven or dark night fills the sky, the priest himself dreads their approach and fears to surprise the lord of the grove.

Lucan uses his poetic licence – not to mention a vivid imagination! – to convey the awe and sense of mystery with which ancient people viewed such places. Other writers confirm his testimony. The Roman historian Tacitus reports 'groves devoted to barbarous and superstitious rites' on Anglesey, where 'altars were honoured with the blood of prisoners and the gods consulted through human entrails'. These holy places were defended against the legions in AD 60 or 61 by 'a densely packed body of armed men, with women running among them, dressed in funeral robes like furies, their hair streaming and with torches in their hands, while druids stood around, raising their hands to heaven and calling down terrible curses'.

Nothing survives of Celtic sacred groves above ground, of course, but offerings were often buried in pits or shafts, or thrown into springs, rivers, lakes or bogs, and these deposits can yield rich rewards when we stumble upon them today. These are offerings to 'chthonic' deities – those believed to reside underground or in the waters. Instead of burnt offerings rising to heaven or precious items pinned to trees, gifts for the gods were passed down to the underworld.

At Geneva, an inlet from the lake contained human remains, especially skulls, and a massive statue carved from oak, perhaps a cult image of the deity that had once dominated a sanctuary on the shore. Many prestige objects have been fished from the Thames – including the Battersea Shield, the Wandsworth Shield-boss and the Waterloo Horned Helmet – while at Llyn Cerrig Bach on Anglesey a rich haul of Iron Age metalwork included a slave-chain. In another peat bog, at Lindow in Cheshire, the offering – perhaps at a moment of supreme crisis – had been an aristocratic man. The flesh survived as leather, even some of the hair remained, and his finely manicured fingernails showed no evidence of manual labour. He had been thrice killed – by a blow to the head, a cut across the throat and strangulation. At Danebury hill-fort in Hampshire, victims had been stoned to death in ritual pits. At Snettisham in Norfolk, there were 12 pits with dozens of gold, electrum,

Above: One of the ritual pits filled with golden torcs at Snettisham in Norfolk - part of the greatest Iron Age treasure ever discovered in Britain.

silver and bronze torcs – but despite intensive search, no evidence was ever found there for a temple, a boundary or any other feature. 'The sheer concentration of material in a small area,' explains Barry Cunliffe, 'and certain details of deposition … leave little doubt that the motive for deposition was ritual. Snettisham with its apparent lack of boundary features and absence of structures, other than votive deposits, provides a fascinating insight into the kind of 'natural' sacred place implied by certain of the classical texts. It is tempting to see

Snettisham as little more than a clearing in a forest protected only by its sanctity and religious taboos restraining the people.'

The field of coins found by Ken Wallace in Leicestershire may have had a sacred boundary. But quite possibly it was no more than a clearing in the forest where wooden idols stood. It would have been an awesome place, avoided except on festival days when some kind of procession would come there, white-robed druids would perform their holy rites and a little pit would be filled with an offering of gold and silver. Perhaps the low hill-crest at the top of the field in Hampshire where Kevan Halls found the golden torcs, brooches, bracelets and chain was also such a place. Most of the field is on chalk, but the highest part is capped with clay-with-flints: harder to work and perhaps left alone by ancient farmers. A patch of wilderness thick with trees and undergrowth that belonged to a god. A place where precious things might pass from the world of men to a realm beyond – from the kings, druids and warrior nobles of Late Iron Age Britain to 'the lord of the grove', a god 'grim and rude'.

4 Roman Burials and Celtic Temples

Previous page: Housesteads Roman fort on Hadrian's Wall, the nothernmost frontier of the Roman Empire.

Below: Part of the 'Romanized' landscape of towns and villas that grew up south of Hadrian's Wall – an artist's reconstruction of the forum at Verulamium (modern St Albans).

Roman Burials and Celtic Temples

When Dave Phillips walked up to the reception desk at the Verulamium Museum in St Albans with his shoebox full of finds on 19 March 2002, the custodians on duty were not overly impressed.

'Is there an archaeologist I can speak to?'

'I'm afraid there's no one in today.'

'Are you sure? I think someone might want to see these.' Then Dave took the lid off the box. One of the custodians picked up the phone immediately. Within ten minutes, Dave and his box were at the centre of a crowd of excited archaeologists and curators who had appeared from various parts of the 'empty' museum. Soon afterwards, field archaeologist Simon West got a call from the museum director: he *had* to come into the museum immediately – a Roman cremation had been found, and a bloke had brought the finds in, and he ought to have a look, and it was really something … A Roman cremation? Simon had spent the last dozen or so years – most of his archaeological career – in St Albans. A Roman cremation here was nothing to get excited about. Verulamium had been the third largest town in Roman Britain. It was surrounded by Roman cemeteries. Some had been excavated, in whole or in part, but there were probably thousands of burials still in the ground. Despite the fact that new planning applications were routinely checked by archaeologists, developers sometimes made unexpected discoveries. Probably, Simon guessed, a digger driver had hit something, and there were a couple of smashed-up pots and some burnt bone. Not exactly the find of the century.

In fact, Simon West was so amazed by what he saw in Dave's shoebox that he was not able to sleep that night – or the following one. There had been a handle in the form of a phallus from a bronze libation vessel, and a beautifully carved head of the goddess

Minerva, also from a handle. And Dave Phillips had said that this was probably only a small part of it, that there was probably much more still in the ground. So Simon and district archaeologist Ros Niblett had been out that very afternoon in the pouring rain to see the holes. They both knew what had to be done. But it would be a couple of days before an emergency excavation team could be organized.

Life in Roman Hertfordshire

Verulamium is one of the best places in Britain to study everyday life in the Roman Empire. In the north and the west, where the army was stationed defending the frontiers, the population was too scattered and impoverished to build many towns or villas. South-east of an imaginary diagonal line from Exeter to York, however, Roman civilization really took off, with around 20 big towns, up to 100 smaller ones and perhaps as many as 1,000 villas. And Verulamium in Hertfordshire, about 25 miles north-west of London, was in the heart of it. Here, for about 300 years, from the late first century AD to the late fourth, the fashionable thing to do among people of property was to live like Romans. If you were a local landowner – and land was the only sort of property that really counted – you built yourself a villa on your estate and a posh house in the local town.

Above: A miniature head decorates the handle of one of the bronze jugs from the Wheathampstead burials.

A place like Gorhambury villa a mile or so outside Verulamium, for instance, or Building XXI.2, a town house (what Romans would have called a *domus*) close to the forum.

Let us picture Gorhambury villa in the late second century AD. There was a small projecting wing at either end of the principal range of rooms, along the front of which ran the main access-corridor. This was a completely new style for domestic buildings. Even the grandest Iron Age chieftain had lived in an open-plan round-house, whereas now the élite were building themselves large, symmetrical, rectangular mansions, with suites of private rooms linked by corridors. Everything about the decoration was new, too, with mosaics,

frescoes on wall plaster, and figured stuccowork which involved moulding relief-sculptures in a fine white plaster. The villa even had its own bath-house.

Above: The Lion and Stag mosaic from Building XXI.2 at Verulamium. It is part of a whole new style in élite living.

Gorhambury villa was close to town. Probably the owners lived there all the time. Usually villas were at a greater distance, in which case life in the Roman style demanded that one also had a town house. Thus a gentleman could combine occasional residence at his country seat – a place of relaxation and leisure (what the Romans called *otium*) – with occasional residence in town, where he would attend to public and business affairs (*negotium*). Contemporary with Gorhambury villa was Building XXI.2. It had at least 14 rooms and corridors, some with tessellated floors and painted plaster, organized as three wings around a central courtyard. The design had all the advantages Roman estate agents admired. Apart from the usual impression of good order implicit in the symmetry of straight lines and sharp angles, it was self-contained and secluded. Shutting out the public world of the streets beyond, the house achieved privacy by looking in on itself: the courtyard would have been laid out as a formal garden, there were covered corridors on three sides of this, and all the rooms in the ranges behind opened into these corridors. The domestic architecture of town and country signifies a revolution in manners. Rooms were partitioned off and, because of corridors, were not needed as walk-throughs. There was an escape from general household to-ing and fro-ing. The change from the noisy intimacy of the Iron Age round-house to the private seclusion of the Roman residence implies a new concept of individualism.

In spite of this, these new Roman houses were still intended for display. They were galleries for showing off the latest fashion in art.

Below: Reconstructed wall fresco from Building XXI.2. It symbolizes wholesale adoption of Mediterranean culture by the British upper classes.

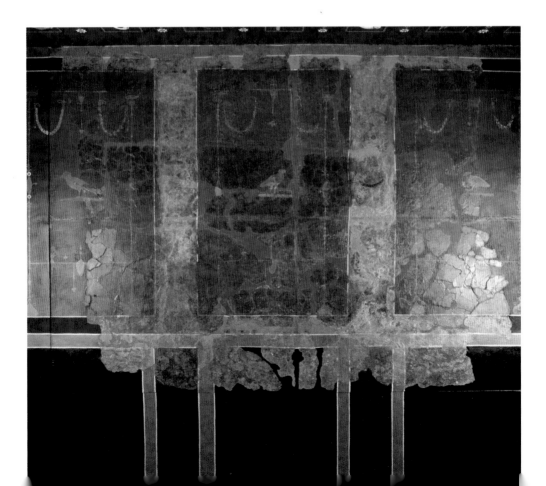

In the well-preserved south-west wing of Building XXI.2 there were some splendid frescoes and mosaics (now superbly displayed in the Verulamium Museum). The corridor walls included red panels decorated with yellow candelabra, blue and yellow swags, and green doves on perches. Reconstruction of fallen ceiling-plaster has revealed a coffer design, like an overhead garden trellis, decorated with birds and feline heads. In the main living room there was a very fine mosaic panel, comprising borders of 'guilloche' (a kind of twisted rope pattern), flower and wine-cup decoration, and a vivid image of a lion holding in its jaws a stag's head dripping blood. The contrast with the Iron Age art discussed in Chapters 1 and 3 could hardly be more extreme: in place of abstract designs of intertwining curves and loops, there was a naturalistic tradition – one which, as it were, 'held up a mirror to nature' – showing plants, animals and people as they really appeared to the eye. The old art was probably now seen as *barbaricus* ('barbarian') and *sine dignitate* ('lacking in sophistication'), whereas the new represented *Romanitas* ('Roman culture'), which was associated with classical education, membership of the élite, Graeco-Roman civilization and the power of the Roman Empire.

The Romanization of Britain

All this does not mean that the owners of these houses were foreigners – or even the descendants of foreigners. Most were Romanized Britons. There was no flood of colonial settlers into Britain after the Roman invasion of AD 43. In so far as there *were* foreigners in the island, the majority of these were soldiers, and most of them had moved west or north after the first few years to the areas where the fighting now was. Behind the advancing frontiers, the foreigners were a handful – the governor, the *procurator* (or finance officer), a modest staff of officials and clerks in London, and small detachments of soldiers acting as guards and policemen. The only major exceptions were the *coloniae* – the colonies of demobbed Roman soldiers established at Colchester, Gloucester and Lincoln. Otherwise, authority remained in local hands. Right across the empire, and for hundreds of years, the Roman policy had been to win over the local landowning élite, encourage it to 'Romanize' and turn it into a class of safe, conservative, small-town politicians. It was local government on the cheap. All the emperor's officials required was that order should be maintained and the taxes collected on time; and the most efficient way to ensure this happened was to use established local dignitaries. We have preserved a speech in praise of Rome delivered by a sycophantic Greek aristocrat called Aelius Aristides around AD 150. He sums up neatly the advantages to the Roman Empire of working through people like himself:

> You have no need to garrison their [the native people's] citadels; the greatest and most powerful men everywhere guard their native places for you … There is no envy at large in your empire. You have set an example in being without envy yourselves by throwing open all doors and offering to qualified men the opportunity to play in turn a ruler's part no less than a subject's … Thus, towns are free from garrisons, and whole provinces are adequately guarded by mere battalions and cavalry companies …

Put simply, the Romans offered the rich a deal because it was in their interests to do so. Co-operate and your property and position are safe. Help us preserve the *status quo*, and you can join us in the privileges of Roman citizenship. You can become, in fact, fully Roman and rise to the highest rank. All this was absolutely true. For the pro-Roman rich, the empire offering dazzling opportunities to ascend the social hierarchy and perhaps reach the very top. There were second-century emperors from Spain and Africa, and in the third century emperors from every corner of the empire. 'You often command our legions in person,' explained the Roman general Petilius Cerialis to an assembly of Gallic nobles in AD 70, 'and in person govern these and other provinces. There is no question of segregation and exclusion … if the Romans are expelled, what else will result but a world-wide war … yours will be the most dangerous situation, for you have the riches and resources which are the main causes of war. At present, victors and vanquished enjoy peace and imperial citizenship on an equal footing, and it is upon these blessings that you must lavish your affection and respect. Learn from your experience of the two alternatives not to choose insubordination and ruin in preference to obedience and security.' Most, faced with the choice between war against the odds and comfortable security, opted for an easy life under the *Pax Romana*. The descendants of moustachioed, blue-painted, beer-swilling Celtic warlords chose to become Roman gentlemen.

The way it worked was as follows. A census was held every four years. All those above a certain minimum wealth assessment were rated as 'decurions' – town councillors – and from their ranks 'magistrates' were elected each year to serve as mayors, judges, city treasurers and clerks of public works. Many were eager to do so. Holding public office was an honour, an opportunity to parade one's aristocratic rank by playing the role of community benefactor. The Roman senator and historian Tacitus viewed it all with a cynical eye:

> Agricola [governor of Britain in AD 78–84] had to deal with men who, because they lived in the country and were culturally backward, were inveterate warmongers. He wanted to accustom them to peace and leisure by providing delightful distractions ... He gave personal encouragement and public assistance to the building of temples, piazzas and town-houses ... he gave the sons of the aristocracy a liberal education ... they became eager to speak Latin effectively ... and the toga was everywhere to be seen ... And so they were gradually led into the decadent vices of porticoes, baths and grand dinner parties. The naïve Britons described these things as 'civilization', when in fact they were simply part of their enslavement.

The Heyday of Verulamium

Notice the link between towns and civilization. For Tacitus, a Roman gentleman, country life, cultural backwardness and warmongering went hand in hand. You needed towns to civilize people – that was where, amid the temples and piazzas, you tried to learn Latin, stumbled around in a toga and generally became decadent. Towns like Verulamium seem, in fact, to have developed in two clear stages. First, between c AD 75 and 150, most of the public buildings were put up. A famous stone inscription records the opening of Verulamium's town hall (*basilica*) in AD 79 or 81. The present-day museum lies on top of the building, parts of which have in the past been excavated, revealing it to be large and rectangular, probably with a nave and two aisles like a traditional church, and a row of offices down the long side which faced the street. The other long side opened on to the forum, an extensive paved open space with colonnaded walkways, and rows of shops around the edge. There were also temples on the far side of the forum opposite the town hall,

Above: The Roman forum at Verulamium in its late-second-century prime. The three buildings along the façing portico were probably temples. They stood opposite the town hall, from which this view is taken.

probably with dedications to Rome's patron deities – Jupiter, Juno and Minerva – and such official 'gods' as *Roma* (a divine personification of the city), and to various dead emperors and the 'spirit' (*genius*) of the living one. The whole town-hall complex was probably plastered and whitewashed on the outside, and had tessellated floors, frescoed walls, marble veneers, stucco mouldings, ornate column capitals and painted stone statues of the great and good on the inside. The place was a monument to civic pride and *Romanitas*. It was a statement of the governing élite's orthodoxy and loyalty to Rome. And, from a practical point of view, it was the place from which the whole surrounding territory was governed. Here magistrates had offices, councillors could hold their meetings, court cases would be heard, and there was plenty of space for local records – including the all-important census and tax records. In a sense, the empire boiled down to a system for creaming off tax revenues from the hinterland to pay the soldiers guarding the frontiers. Coin specialists talk about a 'tax–pay' cycle: coins constantly circulated as people paid taxes, the government paid soldiers, and soldiers paid traders in local markets. But there was nothing inevitable about it. The system was based on force. Most country people were more or less self-sufficient, and anything they did not produce themselves they could get by barter from neighbours, village craftworkers or itinerant traders. They had to be forced to market a surplus in return for coin and then hand over that coin to the state. The towns were the places where this was organized. At the end of the Roman period, the army withdrew, the towns collapsed and country people stopped paying taxes: it all happened as part of the same process. The towns were the bolts that attached the imperial machine to the hundred thousand villages that fuelled it.

Other public buildings also went up in the first two or three generations after Verulamium was founded. In the town centre, close to the forum, there was a sizeable municipal theatre designed to accommodate both stage and arena entertainments. You can still go and see the stone-revetted earth banks on which the seats were placed, the open circle in the middle where animal-baiting and the occasional gladiatorial contest may have taken place, and the raised stage, with one column re-erected as a symbol of past grandeur, on which visiting troupes of players may have performed or religious pageants been enacted. Ancient theatres were probably places of entertainment *and* ritual. Adjacent to the Verulamium theatre, and on the same alignment, was a large rectangular sanctuary with a temple in the middle. The temple was 'Romano-Celtic' – a Roman version in stone and tiles of an earlier, Iron Age design in timber. It consisted of a square central chamber, housing a cult statue and the temple treasures, surrounded by a colonnaded walkway. The deities worshipped in such temples were probably local and Celtic. The Romans did not interfere with native religion provided it was not politically subversive, and very often their own deities were equated with local ones. Celtic cult survived but was 'Romanized'. On the opposite side of the theatre from the temple, just across the main road through the city, was another prominent public building: a purpose-built, pedestrianized shopping mall (*macellum*). Elsewhere, there were more temples, including one of curious triangular design, a large government guest-house (or *mansio*) for official visitors and at least three bath-houses. All these buildings were constructed on the grand scale and sumptuously decorated. They provided the essential settings for living life in a fully Roman way. The Verulamium élite, in providing their town with a complete suite of public buildings similar to those found across the empire, were declaring their membership of the New World Order. This done, they set about building themselves luxurious town houses. Most of these were erected in the next two or three generations – between *c* AD 150 and 225 – by which time Verulamium was at its peak: a flourishing centre of classical civilization on the fringe of the Roman Empire.

Dave Phillips appeared to have stumbled on the burial plot of one of the great families that had ruled the town at the time.

The Wheathampstead Burials

Semi-retired and with worn-out joints after 40 years as a carpet fitter, Dave 'lives and breathes' his hobby. He had started in the 1970s, but for many years had only gone out with his detector occasionally, and had stopped altogether after his son managed to snap the machine in half one day. Much later his partner, Carol Isles, decided he needed a hobby and went out with him to buy a new detector. That was 11 years ago. He still cannot get enough of it. Simon West was not the only one with sleeping problems. When Dave found the Wheathampstead burials two days before he took his shoebox of finds into the Verulamium Museum, he too had sleepless nights.

I couldn't stop thinking: what's in the ground there? I've never had an experience like it. It was better than sex! Totally fulfilling. And it's nothing to do with money. Everyone was asking: how much will you get? When the valuation was done, friends said it should have been more. But it's finding it that matters. The historical interest outstrips any financial gain. 'Treasure trove' is a terrible way to describe it – it should be 'history trove'. It's the knowledge that counts. Both Carol and I have got really into archaeology, and it's been brilliant learning so much from the different experts.

Dave is true to his word. At the coroner's inquest, held to determine whether a find is considered by law to be treasure, there was a tedious argument about whether the two find-spots several yards apart counted as one discovery or two. Did it matter? Well, under the new Treasure Act (see pages 173–82), yes. The problem was that there were two burials, both discovered by Dave, and rich finds had come from both. However, only one of them had contained bullion – two silver brooches and a silver connecting chain. Now, under the law, everything found with these also counted as treasure. But if the burial without bullion was treated as a separate discovery, it would not be treasure. Roman bronze jugs did not count: base-metal artefacts only counted if they were prehistoric in date. The coroner seemed to be enjoying it all. He liked history and the archaeological argument was fun. The hearing continued for two hours. It was finally too much for Dave, who burst out, 'For goodness sake! You can't split them up. It would be a crime. They obviously belong together. Treat them all as treasure!' The coroner thanked him and asked why he had not volunteered this opinion earlier in the proceedings.

Dave had found the site by chance on a carpet-fitting job. He had gone out to Wheathampstead, a village about 10 miles north-east of St Albans, and his client turned out to be one of the biggest landowners in the area. Dave took his chance and got permission to detect. It came with a dampener. Dave was welcome to go out and find whatever he liked, but other detectorists had been trying for years and had never found anything worthwhile. Nor did Dave for some 18 months, at which point, meeting the landowner again by chance, it was suggested that he might try 'the Roman field'. The Roman field?

A pipeline had been laid across the field five years before. There are always pipelines going in somewhere, and they are bread and butter for digging archaeologists. Because you get a great, long, deep trench, sometimes

Above and below: The elegant and beautifully decorated bronze jugs, part of the vast hoard of the Wheathampstead burials, were probably made in Southern Italy.

running for miles, there is a good chance of seeing some archaeology somewhere. So with a pipeline you usually have a 'watching brief' – one or two archaeologists regularly visit the site to check what is in the trench – occasional salvage work, when the machine brings up something unexpected, and often some proper rescue excavation where it is known in advance that the line will pass through a site. In this case, the pipeline investigation had shown that there was a bit of everything – Iron Age, Roman, Anglo-Saxon – including a Roman masonry building. Even so, when Dave first started detecting on the field he found nothing. It happened on the second visit.

Dave was there with his detecting partner, Colin Tillcock. Most detectorists work with at least one other person, partly for company, partly for security. To spend hours on your own in the middle of a ploughed field, especially in dodgy weather, can be a bit demoralizing, and also a bit risky. If you *did* go into a ditch and break your ankle, and if you *were* out of sight and earshot, it could be really nasty. So Colin was there as usual, and he was the one who got the first bit of broken bronze pot, detecting about 100 feet from where the pipeline had gone in. He showed it to Dave, who said he should try for more, but got no more signals and soon gave up. Dave was more determined. He went to work on the find-spot and carried on for a full half-hour without a result. Eventually he got the faintest of signals.

The Truth about Metal-detecting

One of many myths about metal-detectors is that you can 'strip a field' of artefacts in a day. The truth is that most artefacts are so small that you only get a signal if they are within a few inches of the surface, and even then you've got to sweep directly above them. The search-head must be kept flat and as close to the ground as possible – if you are not constantly scuffing the ground and wearing out the machine's underside, you are not using it properly. To cover ground thoroughly takes a long time. You could cross the same patch a dozen times and on the thirteenth still find a target you have missed.

It took a bit of time to get down to the burial as it was over 2 feet from the surface. The first thing Dave noticed was something that looked like a Roman brooch, only it was five times too big. It was actually a jug handle. Then it became clear that there were several objects – some bronze, some glass. A second signal a few yards away was also investigated, and this too was found to come from not one but an entire assemblage of objects. At this point Dave phoned the farmer, who promptly arrived and volunteered his JCB to complete the excavation. It was a slightly awkward moment. How do you tell the landowner on whose land you are working not to bring in his JCB? Especially when shortly afterwards you find two silver brooches, and it is obvious that there is still loads more down there. Two things can go wrong in this situation. The idea that you stand to make a fortune can take over: a voice says, 'Dig it out, do not tell anyone, flog it for as much as you can get.' But that is not what drives most metal-detectorists. Some people are greedy, but most are not, and for them the appeal is the excitement of discovery, of finding out what is there, of being in contact with a past that has not been touched for 2,000 years. It was the greatest discovery Dave had ever made, he had only seen a small bit of it, and it took tremendous self-control for him not to dig out the whole lot straight away. The key thing was this: whatever was there, it was *in situ*. There were two groups of intact objects lying together just as they had been left by the people who put them there in the Roman period. It was pretty obvious what these deposits had to be. On settlement sites, you get smashed-up rubbish. In hoards and ritual deposits, you get coins, bullion, metalwork, high-value offerings. These objects had to be grave-goods – which meant that this was the burial place of some of the richest people around in Roman Hertfordshire.

Assessing the Fields

For both Dave Phillips and Simon West the big worry, especially given that they were in the heavily populated commuter belt north of London, was that the site was visible and accessible from local roads. The danger of a raid was real – whether the casual rummaging of local kids or a professional attack by nighthawks. It was vital to get the material out as quickly as possible.

In fact, once a dig started and drew attention to the site, anything of value would have to be got out on the first day. Simon had seen Dave's finds in the museum on the Tuesday. By the Friday he had a team on site, and by that evening, with darkness falling, they had taken out all the non-ferrous metalwork picked up by the detectors, along with any other objects exposed while they were digging. They were back on Saturday and Sunday to remove the iron objects, excavate the cremations and record the two pits in which the burials had been placed. The haul of grave-goods was astonishing. There was a total of 153 separate items, including 13 bronze vessels, among them the phallic libation-pourer and the jug whose handle had been decorated with a head of Minerva, 14 Samian vessels (fine tableware with a red glossy surface), 9 glass vessels, 3 iron blades, 2 silver brooches (decorated with sea serpents) with their connecting chain, a bronze lamp-holder, bronze fittings from a wooden casket, and a bag full of huntsmen's arrowheads.

Right: Dave Phillips (foreground) on the excavation led by Simon West (standing behind, looking down the trench).

It was a top of the range assemblage which demanded detailed specialist work. Among those called in was Martin Henig.

Martin is an Oxford don with a mane of wild white hair which matches his flamboyant enthusiasm for classical art. His admiration for the Romans is unashamedly eccentric and élitist: classical culture, he maintains, required intellectual effort and was therefore something principally for 'the educated, more or less well-to-do, and above all Romanized section of society'. 'I am sorry if this is "politically incorrect",' he explains with an air of injured innocence, 'but my theme is largely concerned with provincial Roman culture and not those left outside it.' Confronted by the Wheathampstead finds, Martin was in his element: this was *better* than 'Roman provincial art', some of it at least, since the grave-goods included quality Italian bronze flagons such as you might have seen in the grandest of Pompeian town houses before the city's destruction in AD 79. The decoration on the handles included miniature faces and figures in the best naturalistic tradition of classical art: a Minerva (goddess of wisdom), a triton (a mythic male mermaid) and a Medusa (the ghastly gorgon whose gaze turned men to stone). 'These bronzes were the finest money could buy anywhere in the Roman Empire,' Martin says. 'They were probably imported from Italy by sea and entered the province through the port of

London. They might have travelled up Watling Street to Verulamium, or perhaps they were purchased on a shopping spree in the provincial capital.' The Samian ware was imported from Gaul, the glassware probably from the Rhineland, and

Right: Hidden Treasure *presenter Miranda Krestovnikoff finds Oxford don and Roman art expert Martin Henig exploring a 'hobbit hole'.*

there were also pieces of ivory, the most exotic and expensive of materials. 'Ivory puts the burials in a different league altogether. Ivory is very rare. And to burn or bury ivory – to consume it in a funerary rite – is the height of super-rich ostentation.' The ivory may have been a name plaque fastened to the wooden casket in which one of the cremations had been placed. There were also decorative iron rings and a corroded lump of iron which may have been the lock. The cremation in the other grave, which had far fewer grave-goods, had been placed in a large, square, green-glass urn.

The emergency dig to rescue the grave-goods, essential though it was, had left the two burials floating in a vacuum. Were there any more – were they part of a larger cemetery? Were there mounds over them or enclosures around them? Were there any structures nearby? What was the relationship between the burials and the Roman building found in the pipeline trench? Simon was determined to find out. Geophysics revealed an area 'stuffed full of archaeology'. A four-week dig in June and July confirmed the pipeline evidence: Iron Age, Roman and Anglo-Saxon activity. Though there were no more burials, a T-junction section of Roman wall may have been part of a mausoleum, perhaps in the form of a temple. Or could it have been part of a villa, albeit lying very close to the burials? Alternatively, there were obscure references in a nineteenth-century gentleman's magazine to the discovery of a Late Roman mosaic a short distance away and in line-of-sight. Could this, perhaps, point to the location of the grand country residence of the people buried here? Certainly they belonged to the highest ranks of the Hertfordshire aristocracy in Roman times. Almost certainly they were Romano-British – not foreigners. There was some ordinary local pottery in the graves, a bronze 'wine strainer' was judged an essentially Iron Age artefact, and the designs on the silver brooches appeared Celtic to some specialists. These were native aristocrats with deep roots in Britain. But they had bought in wholeheartedly to the new Roman style, and Simon was drawn to a comparison with another high-status Hertfordshire burial he had worked on ten years before.

Celtic Survivals

Simon West had been a supervisor on Ros Niblett's excavation of the Folly Lane burial in 1991–3. The site lies a short distance outside Verulamium on a hill to the north-east. The grave-goods dated the burial to the beginning of the Roman period – but there was nothing Roman about the ritual represented. The funeral was a protracted affair, notes Ros Niblett:

> The body had been exposed – for how long we do not know – in a wooden chamber built on the floor of a 10-foot-deep shaft. There was feasting, or at any rate drinking, since fragments of up to seven Italian wine amphorae were found strewn across the shaft floor. Heavily trampled gravel around the chamber implied dancing or ceremonial

processions. Finally the body was taken out and cremated, together with many valuable objects, including an ivory chair or couch, a tunic of chain mail, and a cart or chariot and various items of horse-gear. A small portion of the burnt remains were then buried in a shallow grave beside the funerary shaft. Even this was not quite the end of proceedings. The funerary chamber was smashed up and the shaft filled with earth brought to the site from different locations. We can imagine the local inhabitants bringing earth from their farms and fields to fill the shaft and raise a mound – as symbols, perhaps, of the land once ruled by this Iron Age lord. But the pyre, it seems, mattered more than the grave itself, for this was at the centre of the rectangular ditched enclosure around the site, and was permanently commemorated, first by a large post, then by a small shrine of Romano-Celtic design, such that the monument continued to be venerated for at least 150 years.

Below: A thoroughly Celtic send-off for a high-ranking Brit in Early Roman Verulamium, shown in an artist's reconstruction of the Folly Lane burial.

Surely this was the burial of a Celtic king? The Roman invasion split the Iron Age aristocracy down the middle. Some, like Caratacus and later Boudicca, resisted. Others, like Togidubnus, the

client-king of the Southern Kingdom, and Prasutagus, client-king of the Iceni and Boudicca's husband until his death, co-operated. The Folly Lane man may not have been a client-king, but he must have been an aristocrat of royal rank who had made his peace with Rome, and remained at home in Hertfordshire when others fled west to continue the fight.

Similar burials have been found elsewhere. At the Stanway cemetery just outside Colchester, Philip Crummy found a complex of five large rectangular enclosures containing sunken chambers and rich burials, all of first-century date, some definitely post-Conquest. These, too, must have been royal burials, and the latest of them is evidence of a pro-Roman stance. A hundred years later, however, these 'barbarian' rites have disappeared and the top aristocracy has fully 'Romanized'. The Wheathampstead burials belong to the later second century. We can imagine the people buried in such 'civilized' style as toga-clad politicians on walkabout in Verulamium's forum. Their transition from chariot-borne Celtic warlords was complete. Roman Britain was in safe hands.

Beneath the surface, however – beneath that veneer of classical culture in which the top ranks dressed their world – an older, deep-rooted, indigenous culture survived. It is unfashionable to call this culture 'Celtic'. This was a term used by Greek and Roman enemies, for whom so-called 'Celts' or 'Gauls' were archetypal barbarians, and recently it has been hijacked by Breton, Cornish, Welsh, Scottish and Irish nationalists, whose proclaimed 'Celtic' national identities are in fact modern inventions. Yet those who wish to 'deconstruct' false historical categories sometimes go too far. Archaeology and linguistics show that there was a baby in the bath: a common material culture and a common language unites the late prehistoric populations of that huge swathe of northern and western Europe that classical writers describe as 'Celtic'. Leading prehistorian Barry Cunliffe is insistent about the real existence of the ancient Celts:

It could be argued that biased historical anecdotes, ill-understood patterns of early language development and hard archaeological 'facts' – the artefacts, ecofacts and structures of the past recovered through excavation – should not, and indeed cannot, be brought together to create a coherent picture of the past. The position is firmly taken by some and energetically argued; it is not one with which I have much sympathy. Given an array of disparate evidence, we would, I believe, be failing if we were to fight shy of the challenges posed by using every available scrap in our attempt to construct a European protohistory. In doing so we will, inevitably, be drawn into simplification and generalization, laying ourselves open to criticism from the purists, but better the attempt to create a whole, however imperfect, than to be satisfied with the minute examination of only a part.

Whatever they called themselves, whatever divisions existed among them, the Celts were in some sense real, and Celtic culture provided an alternative symbolic 'language' for describing the world and people's place within it. An alternative, that is, to the dominant classical culture of the élite. Cultural identities form and re-form, endure or disappear, in conflict with other, rival, identities. We define ourselves as 'normal' and others as 'different'. Cultures are always at root about recognizing and marking out differences. They become, therefore, a way of expressing social tensions.

Not everyone in Roman Britain bought into classical 'civilization'. Not everyone was a 'stakeholder'. There were also losers: principally the mass of country people for whom Rome meant taxation and labour service. The peasantry were the pack animals on which the 'civilization' of towns, villas and the army rested. In the villages, hamlets and farmsteads where most people lived, a traditional, pre-Roman, indigenous culture seems to have endured, one only partly visible in an archaeological record dominated by the rich and powerful. *Roman* Britain was also very much *Celtic* Britain. It still contained the raw materials for preserving – or refashioning – a different cultural identity from that of the conquerors: the Celtic language with its bards, myths and fairy tales; the native landscape with its local gods and sacred groves; the traditional patterns and motifs of folk art; even the taken-for-granted routines and customs of everyday life in peasant settlements. In searching out this cultural underbelly, it is in the archaeology of religion in Roman Britain that we find our best evidence.

The Baldock Hoard

Gil Burleigh was doing the washing-up midway through a Sunday morning when he got the call. He had recently taken early retirement after almost 30 years in the North Hertfordshire Museums Service. During his time there he had pioneered building good relationships with local detectorists. From as far back as 1976 he had taken a wholly pragmatic view of matters.

Of course you came across some unscrupulous people from time to time, and of course some finds went unrecorded, however hard you tried. But many detectorists were only too keen to be hooked up with the archaeologists in the museums service, and there was lots of useful data to be collected. The recording rate had shot up a couple of times in the previous ten years. The last occasion was in the late 1990s, with the new Treasure Act and the start of the Portable Antiquities Scheme (see page 181). Prior to that, in the early 1990s, it had gone up when Andy Phillips set up a new detecting club – the North Hertfordshire Charity Detecting Group (NHCDG) – with which Gil had developed an especially close relationship. Andy's group, which was small but active, went out most Sundays, and the proceeds from the sale of any find were split three ways between the finder, the landowner and a charity. Despite formal retirement, Gil was still a very busy archaeologist. In fact, he remained at the centre of a web of contacts linking metal-detectorists, the amateur archaeologists of the North Hertfordshire Archaeological Society, the museums service and Heritage Network, the local professional digging unit run by David Hillelson. If anything moved in North Herts archaeology, Gil was probably involved. He was the main man.

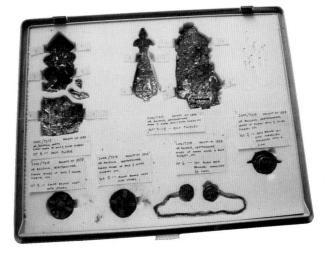

Above: Part of the Baldock hoard on display, showing gold and silver votive plaques, round brooches (one pair with chain) and a gold clasp.

Left: Close-up of the gold clasp with its intact carnelian intaglio depicting a proud lion, one of the best preserved of its type.

That is why he got the call. It was Andy Phillips, phoning on his mobile from a field somewhere near Baldock.

'Gil, we've found something very exciting. We think it's very significant. We've found what is definitely a hoard. There are gold leaves, bronze leaves, gold jewellery and a silver figurine. The jewellery includes brooches. And one item has an intaglio with a lion on it. It's Roman. Can you come out straight away and record the finds?'

Gil was on site with his recording gear before the end of the morning. He had asked that digging should stop so he could record stuff *in situ* when he got there, but much had already been taken out by the time of the phone call. It was laid out on Alan Meek's yellow jumper beside the hole when Gil arrived. There were a dozen people gathered there in the middle of the field, but Alan was the finder. A retired Fleet Street photographer, Alan came up from Putney to North Herts most Sundays to work as part of Andy's detecting group. That took commitment: on a bad day it could mean several hours in cold and rain on a muddy field followed by sometimes three hours nose to tail in the late Sunday traffic back across London. But Alan had the bug, the NHCDG were a nice bunch, and it was hassle-free because Andy arranged everything with the local farmers. All you had to do was turn up with your detector and pay a small sub which went to charity.

Gil tried to stay calm when he saw what was on Alan's sweater, but it required self-control. He had been digging for 40 years – ever since working, aged 13, on a site in Southwark looking for Shakespeare's Swan Theatre – but he had never seen anything like this. The detectorists were sure there was more in the hole as they were all getting signals, and it was vital to get everything out and the basic recording done by the end of the day. Gil had a chat with the group, explaining that the finds would fall under the Treasure Act, that the British Museum would have to be brought in, and that it was necessary to clean up the hole and make sure every fragment was recovered. They searched for an hour. Because different machines get different results – as sometimes different operators do with the same machine – every bit of spoil was swept repeatedly for signals. They also sieved it and picked out small pieces by hand. But there were no more complete objects, just broken fragments. Gil, meantime, having cleaned up and recorded the find-spot, called up further help: David Hillelson, the head of Heritage Network, arrived with his partner Helen Ashworth to produce a digitized photographic record and help stabilize and package the finds. David, though he headed a commercial unit that had to pay its way, was another part of Gil Burleigh's informal North Herts network. His unit had close links with Gil and the local amateurs, and was often involved in community projects.

They finished at dusk. Three days later, Gil Burleigh and Alan Meek arrived in central London with the finds and handed them over to Ralph Jackson, one of the British Museum's leading Roman experts.

A New Celtic Goddess

When Ralph wrote his official report for the Hertfordshire coroner, he knew he was dealing with a 'structured deposit'. Alan had been able to report that the finds had been arranged in the ground in a compact and ordered manner. At the top had been the 6-inch silver figurine of a standing woman dressed in a full-length garment, her left shoulder bare, her left arm supporting a fold of drapery. Her condition was poor: much of the figure was corroded, distorted or broken away, and it was impossible to say who she was meant to be. Then came the gold jewellery – a pair of disc brooches, a pair of discs linked by a chain, and a gold clasp set with a red carnelian gemstone engraved with a standing lion resting his paw on a bull's head or ox skull. With the gold were two silver female arms, one holding a libation vessel, the other a sheaf of corn. Beneath these were seven closely packed gold votive plaques, five of which were still stuck together with a blackish waxy substance. Finally, at the bottom, were 12 silver-alloy votive plaques, all of which were brittle and fragmentary; it was mainly bits broken off these that had continued to give detector signals after Alan had removed all the intact objects from the hole. The group had all the appearance of a deliberate votive deposit, but what put this beyond all reasonable doubt were the images and inscriptions on the plaques. What these also did, almost certainly, was reveal the identity of the silver woman at the top of the pile.

Above: The silver figurine discovered by Alan Meek as part of the Baldock hoard, later identified as Senua, a Romano-British goddess.

'The 19 plaques were of a type known from other sites in Roman Britain and elsewhere in the Roman Empire,' explains Ralph Jackson. 'They are made from very thin sheet-metal, with embossed and incised decoration, and were intended for dedication at a temple or shrine, to one or more gods or goddesses.' Twelve of Alan's plaques had embossed images of a deity, and all bar one were depictions of the classical goddess Minerva. Several of the plaques also had inscriptions, however, and on all five where the goddess was named the

Above: Ralph Jackson, one of the British Museum's leading Roman experts, discusses the Baldock finds with series presenter Miranda Krestovnikoff.

dedication was not to Roman Minerva, but to a previously unknown Celtic deity called Senua. 'Lucilia willingly and deservedly fulfils her vow to the goddess Senua,' says one. 'Servandus willingly fulfils his vow to the goddess Senua,' declare two others. 'The combination of the name Senua with the image of Minerva would suggest the twinning of a local British deity with the popular Roman goddess of wisdom and the crafts,' says Ralph Jackson. 'Minerva also had warlike protective powers and an association with healing and with springs, as at Bath, where, twinned with Sulis, she controlled Britain's only thermal spring. Senua might have been likened to Minerva for any one, or more, of these perceived powers.'

While Ralph Jackson worked on the finds at the British Museum, Gil Burleigh was busy in North Hertfordshire organizing a collaborative field project for the early spring. He was determined to go back into that field and find a context for Alan's treasure. It was to bring spectacular confirmation of Ralph's guesses about Roman Britain's new goddess Senua-Minerva.

The project involved everyone. The landowner was interested and supportive. Alan, Andy and the rest of the detector club were there. Amateur archaelogists from the North Herts and Stevenage groups volunteered to help. GeoQuest Associates were on site to do the geophysics. Ralph Jackson at the British Museum stayed in close contact. And David Hillelson's Heritage Network provided a professional digging team led by Chris Turner.

Right: Detail of a silvered copper votive plaque showing an embossed image of the goddess Senua-Minerva, found by Alan Meek as part of the Baldock hoard.

The project plan was for three types of field survey followed by some carefully targeted excavation. A grid was laid out across some 10 acres of ground around the find-spot, and fieldwalkers, detectorists and the geophysics team then surveyed it. The fieldwalkers found masses of material, the bulk of it concentrated in certain specific areas – Romano-British pottery, Roman tiles, *tesserae* (cubes from tessellated floors) and bits of *opus signinum* (Roman concrete). In the formal prose of the official report: 'The evidence from the fieldwalking survey shows the presence of an underlying Romano-British settlement. Pottery collected suggests that the site was occupied throughout the Roman period ... The recovery of tile, *tesserae* and *opus signinum* indicates substantial buildings stood in the immediate vicinity.' The metal-detector survey, on the same grid, yielded 55 Roman and two Celtic coins in a few hours. Hundreds of earlier finds had already been logged with Gil by Andy's group. All the finds clustered in certain areas. GeoQuest's geophysics results confirmed the discovery of a major site:

> The evidence ... has revealed part of a long-lived and significant Romano-British settlement, with possible prehistoric origins. The palimpsest of enclosures at the south-eastern end of the gridded area indicates occupation over a relatively long period of time. The line of rectangular enclosures facing on to the trackway and the small circular enclosure opposite, as well as the possible porticoed building, may represent the remains of a street lined on one side with domestic habitation, and on the other with a ritual site and possible official building.

What was most exciting of all was that the 'small circular enclosure' which might be 'a ritual site' was precisely where Alan Meek had found the hoard of gold and silver votive offerings to the goddess Senua. There was no doubt where the trial trenches should go.

Three linked trenches were laid out and a mini-digger was brought in to take the topsoil off about 1,000 square feet in all. Four professionals and about twice that number of volunteers then worked for four days in the damp clay. It was still only an 'evaluation': the job was not to carry out full excavation, but to use a range of techniques, including small, targeted trenches, to get out some basic information. When was the site occupied (date)? What sort of site was it ('characterization')? How well preserved are the archaeological deposits? Are they under any immediate threat (for example, from ploughing)?

Above: Alan Meek (centre) with Carl Skelton (left) and Howard
Hutchins (right) checking for more treasure, with the recovered objects
spread on the yellow jumper in the foreground.

The evaluation was spectacularly successful. It was one of those projects where everything fitted together like a jigsaw puzzle: the hoard, the pottery and metalwork scatters, the crystal-clear geophysics results, well-located trenches, and now first-class features and finds in the excavation. The best find was a small silver statue-base. It was right next to the find-spot of the hoard and was almost certainly the missing base from the silver figurine. It was inscribed: *SENUA*. Close by, the remains of the goddess's shrine were revealed. As the official report puts it:

> The excavation appears to have revealed part of a circular structure or enclosure surrounding a possible springhead, defined by a chalk and mortar foundation. At least one chalk pad was identified within the enclosed area, which may have provided dry standing in the marshy soil and has been interpreted as a platform from which votive offerings were made. The remains of a possible walkway outside the structure were also observed on the western side. Votive deposits, including Bronze Age metalwork, Celtic and Roman coins, parts of several pipeclay figurines, a pig skeleton, other animal bone, iron mail, weapons and personal effects, e.g. brooches, pottery, nails and cremated bone, were also recorded.

It seemed to be an extraordinary confirmation of Ralph Jackson's guess that Senua, because she had been equated with Minerva, may have been a water goddess. There was still an element of uncertainty: there was no spring here now, and the samples taken for analysis by archaeo-environmental specialists had not yet been analysed to show whether or not the ground within the enclosure had been wet in antiquity. But the field was *known* to contain dried-up springs, and there were still streams running either side of it. And there would be nothing out of the ordinary in a pagan water temple: for well over a thousand years, British people had been casting offerings into water, and we know they continued to do this at many sites throughout the Roman period.

The shrine may have been fairly simple, but the richness of the offerings to Senua shows her to have been a deity of at least local importance. The hoard may have been a gathering up and ritual burial by her priests of separate offerings made over a long period. The names of several votaries appear on the inscriptions on the gold and silver plaques: *Cariatia* (or *Cariatus*), *Celsus*, *Firmanus*, *Lucilia*, and *Servandus*. They tell us they were votaries: people who made a vow to the goddess that in return for some favour they would make such-and-such an offering. She may have been a healing goddess – Minerva was often associated with health – and perhaps they prayed for an end to pain or the recovery of a sick child. They would make a

Above: Gil Burleigh discusses the base of the silver statue with Miranda Krestovnikoff.

declaration, a *nuncupatio*, that if the goddess heard their prayer they would set up an altar, sacrifice a pig, or bestow upon her a treasured gold brooch. Our evidence then catalogues the success stories. We see the votive offerings and we read the inscriptions which record acts of *solutio* – a dissolution of the vow by the performance of the promised act – and our votaries tell us that they do this 'willingly and deservedly' for a goddess who must have favoured them. *V S L M*, says Lucilia at the end of the dedication on her silver plaque – that is, *VOTUM SOLVIT LIBENS MERITO*, 'she fulfilled her vow willingly and deservedly'. Perhaps the whole of the settlement around the Sanctuary of Senua had grown up to serve the cult and the pilgrim trade it attracted.

The Sacred Spring of Bath

Of all the sites in Roman Britain which seem to owe their existence to a cult the most famous is Bath. At this extraordinary place, water heated deep beneath the earth's crust gushes to the surface at a rate of a quarter of a million gallons a day. The water has a consistent temperature of 46.5°C. In the Iron Age the area was a steaming marsh, beneath the surface of which resided the great goddess Sulis. In the Roman period the spring was contained within a reservoir, into which vast numbers of holy offerings were cast. Archaeologists led by Barry Cunliffe recovered jewellery and gemstones, pewter jugs and cups, more than 12,000 coins spanning the entire Roman period, and about 90 pewter curse tablets denouncing some malefactor and appealing to the goddess for restitution and justice. But the Sacred Spring was only the central focus of a vast complex laid out around it. On one side was the Sanctuary of Sulis-Minerva, which included a classical-style temple, fronted by a portico with four fluted Corinthian columns and an intricately carved pediment sculpture which was a masterpiece of Romano-British art. On the other side was a huge bathing complex, including a Great Bath into which hot spring water was piped continuously, with full suites of hot, warm and cold rooms at either end. The many inscriptions left by visitors – not only on curse tablets, but on dedicatory altars and tombstones – tell us that pilgrims came here from far and wide, even from beyond the Channel. Roman Bath must have been comparable with medieval Canterbury or modern Lourdes. The little town that grew up here was dominated by the cult complex it served.

Gil Burleigh's site near Baldock was on a relatively modest scale. The pool – if pool it was – had probably been open to the air and, though there was at least one substantial structure nearby, there was no integrated complex of grand buildings. The archaeology of Roman Britain knows of several similar sanctuaries, sometimes in isolated rural locations, sometimes forming parts of larger settlements, and quite often focused on a springhead, a sacred pool and the casting of offerings into the waters. The surveys around the Sanctuary of Senua revealed a trackway with enclosures and buildings on either side of it. These may all be linked with the cult. Perhaps there was accommodation for priests, officials and pilgrims, and various trading establishments selling trinkets, quack remedies and 'personal services'. Or it may be evidence for a substantial

Opposite: The Great Bath at the centre of the Roman religious and bathing complex at Bath in Avon. It was filled by water from a hot spring considered in antiquity to be sacred.

village, many of whose residents were farmers. It is too early to tell. What is clear is that this was not some desolate spot in the wilderness. The market town of Baldock was within walking distance – measured in ancient terms – and the county town of Verulamium was only a day's journey away on the other side of the Chilterns. The countryside in between was dotted with villas and other rural settlements, perhaps one every mile or so, and the landscape must have been as open as today, a scene of rolling arable fields with only occasional patches of woodland.

We know a great deal about the Roman settlement pattern. The province of *Britannia* was divided into tribal territories – or *civitates* – each the size of a large modern county like Norfolk or Yorkshire. These were governed from major urban centres such as Verulamium, where there would be an administration complex – a forum–basilica – in which the district council was based. But there were only about 20 such towns in the whole of Roman Britain, and it was the network of smaller towns like Baldock, places without major governmental responsibilities but with a market and craft workshops, that serviced the local countryside. The settlement hierarchy then graded down into various roadside settlements, villa estate-centres, farming hamlets, industrial villages and rural sanctuaries. Most numerous of all were the very large numbers of individual farmsteads scattered across the landscape. Recent surveys revealing the density of settlement in Roman Britain, at least in the south-eastern lowlands, have forced an upward revision of population estimates: from two or three million to five or six – higher, perhaps, than at any other time before the fourteenth century.

The Ritual Landscape

The settlement pattern is only one possible way of viewing the Romano-British past. It sees the world only in functional terms, as human geography, where the use of the landscape is interpreted as a system of economy and government. There are other ways. There are also landscapes of perception, belief and the divine – the ritual landscapes of past people's imagination. If we want to understand the past, we must operate at different levels: at a modern, functionalist level, where we try to understand how people made a living, how they traded, how they were taxed; but also at an ideological level, where we attempt to reconstruct past thought-worlds and see the landscape revealed by archaeology as it may have been seen by those who lived in it. Even in more secularized modern societies, every village has a church, a mosque or a temple, every town several. Many Catholic countries are filled with wayside shrines, and Middle Eastern ones with the white-domed tombs of martyrs. This was so much more the case in the ancient past, when religion provided not only its own language, but a language for politics and public affairs generally. Everything was discussed in terms of divine judgement, and even the smallest human endeavours were preceded by supplication and sacrifice.

It is easy enough to understand why. Nature was unpredictable and inexplicable. Society was oppressive and cruel. Life was ruled by the terrible tyranny of fate. So men and women imagined all human experience to be governed by a great pantheon of spirit beings. There were thousands of minor spirits who guarded a household, a spring or a clearing in the woods. Some hundreds, perhaps, had developed into more powerful and famous deities, specialists in a particular kind of divine assistance such as healing, success in war, or safety in passage across the sea. A handful had become super-gods, known and worshipped everywhere, notably the great mother-goddesses who presided over the harvest, or the mighty lords of the universe who controlled the elements and the fates. These many gods were quick to anger, but they could be appeased by appropriate ritual and a suitable offering and, if especially honoured, they could be won to active assistance. People lived with the belief that the landscape was populated by spirits, that their own simplest acts were observed, and that for them just to live safely, let alone well, they had to know the sacred places, the laws that governed them, and the holy rites by which the good favour of those who dwelt there might be constantly renewed.

The ritual landscape, though it evolved, was hundreds, maybe thousands, of years old. The newly imported Roman cults were but a thin veneer. These élite cults were richly patronized, of course, and are prominent in the archaeological record. There are municipal temples to Rome's patron deities – Jupiter, Juno and Minerva – worshipped together as the 'Capitoline Triad'. There are official temples dedicated to the deified emperors of the past and the living spirit of the present incumbent. The soldiers worshipped Jupiter *Optimus Maximus* ('Best and Greatest'), Mars, god of war, and of course the emperor, their commander-in-chief. A Roman army officer keen on the chase might be a devotee of the huntress-goddess Diana or of the woodland deity Silvanus. Foreigners were probably more often initiates of one or another of the exotic 'mystery cults' from the East – that of Dionysus, Cybele, Isis, Dolichenus, Mithras or Christ. It seems unlikely, though, that these

alien religions made many converts among the native population. Few tried: most were self-contained and socially exclusive, with no great sense of a mission to convert the benighted. The one supreme exception – Christianity – was also the only one of the new religions that was monotheistic: its proselytizing mission was linked with its conviction that all other gods were false. Pagans were content to live and let live: the special relationship that many of them had with one particular deity did not preclude the validity of other relationships with different deities. The town councillors going through the motions for Jupiter in the local forum, the soldiers up on Hadrian's Wall making sacrifices to Mars, the foreign traders who visited the Temple of Mithras in London, were all probably largely indifferent to the overwhelmingly Celtic ritual landscape that survived outside the Romanized enclaves of town and fort.

Some of the Celtic cults acquired a Roman gloss. The native deity was equated to a Roman equivalent and became Mars-Rigonemetos or Apollo-Maponus. The timber temple was rebuilt in stone. The bog was drained and a layer of hardcore put down. Figurines executed in classical style were ritually installed. Altars inscribed in Latin were erected in fulfilment of vows. But it was only a gloss. These were sacred places and divine entities inherited from the Iron Age past. Even the most elaborate make-over could not obscure the Celtic essence beneath. The Romanization of Celtic cults was nowhere more thorough than at Bath, yet every dedication that has survived gives the goddess's name as Sulis or Sulis-Minerva – but never as plain old Roman Minerva. It was a Celtic incarnation of the divine that people were worshipping. In most cases, so numerous were the minor local deities, so densely settled by spirits was the ritual landscape, that there was hardly any Roman gloss at all. The country people of Roman Britain, like the people of traditional societies throughout history, must have lived out their lives rarely moving more than a few miles in any direction, living in a landscape both human and divine that they had inherited largely unchanged from countless generations of their forebears. The bronze flagons from southern Italy that Dave Phillips found in the Wheathampstead burials open a window on a world of Romanized sophistication at the top of society. But the name on the base of the silver figurine that Alan Meek found in a field near Baldock reveals that the Romano-British lords of Verulamium ruled a world that was still basically Celtic.

5 Mead-halls and Tombs of the Warrior Lords

Mead-halls and Tombs of the Warrior Lords

Dave Cummings sells tropical fish for a living, but he is a ruddy-faced countryman, born and bred in Suffolk, who is happiest when out in the fields with his detector – in one field near Ipswich in particular, as it happens, where he has been working now for 15 years. This seems extraordinary for all sorts of reasons. For a start, when his wife first bought him a metal-detector 30 years ago, he tried it in his garden, concluded it did not work, and left it in a cupboard for six months. It was not that he lacked interest – he had been a coin collector since childhood – but he only got the hang of detecting some time later, working with a friend in a vicarage garden looking for bits and pieces of Victorian rubbish. Then there was the field itself: at first it did not look promising. An experienced team of detectorists had worked over it thoroughly and found nothing. Then when Dave's group started, the first results were negative. He often works with his wife Mary, his son Francis, and his detecting partner Peter Murrell. After several days of finding nothing, Peter was ready to give up, but Dave was determined. He was looking at the lie of the land – a small valley with gentle slopes on either side – and thinking it was a lovely sheltered spot, perfect for a settlement: there had to be one. 'A lot of blokes just can't be bothered,' he says. 'You need patience and persistence. Metal-detectors just aren't that efficient. They can only pick up a small coin at 3 or 4 inches. Some things are incredibly hard to find.'

Above: Dave Cummings shows Miranda Krestovnikoff one of his finds.

Early in 1988, the group got its first finds. Peter found an Anglo-Saxon *sceat* (plural *sceattas*). *Sceattas* are silver coins minted from the 690s and for most of the eighth century. A little later, Peter found another coin, this time a debased *thrymsa* of the later seventh century; and when the team returned to the field after harvest in the autumn, they quickly found more *thrymsas*, including earlier issues with a higher gold content. *Thrymsas* are very rare compared to *sceattas*. They were the first Anglo-Saxon coins minted in England, starting shortly after *c*625, and the early issues were gold. It was Francis, Dave's son, who found the first early *thrymsa*. 'He couldn't believe it,' Dave remembers. 'He wasn't sure what it was, but I knew as soon as I caught sight of it – it was an Anglo-Saxon gold coin.' By now, 'in all this excitement' – as the official coin report laconically remarks – 'it seems that *sceattas* were small beer.'

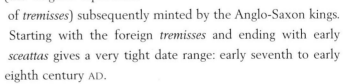

Over succeeding years they kept finding coins, always one at a time, scattered over a large area. Dave knew that because the coins could only be detected when close to the surface, it paid to keep going back year after year as each fresh ploughing would bring new material within range of the machines. The field to date has produced 3 *tremisses* (singular *tremissis*), 12 *thrymsas*, and some 50 early *sceattas*. The *tremisses*, like *thrymsas*, are rare. They are small gold coins minted on the Continent, each one worth a third of a gold piece (or *solidus*), and they were the models for the *thrymsas* (the English equivalent

Upper left: A Merovingian tremissis quarter found by Dave Cummings.

Above: An Anglo-Saxon thrymsa.

Lower left: An Anglo-Saxon sceat, with a 'porcupine' design.

of *tremisses*) subsequently minted by the Anglo-Saxon kings. Starting with the foreign *tremisses* and ending with early *sceattas* gives a very tight date range: early seventh to early eighth century AD.

There are two very puzzling things about all this. First, the sheer quantity of early coins is extraordinary. If Dave's group had been finding eighth-century *sceattas* or ninth-century silver pennies, it would have been an impressive total. But these are seventh-century coins and, says Anglo-Saxon coin specialist Michael Metcalf, 'no other site in England has yielded so many *thrymsas* – indeed, one, or at the most two, is the norm'. Second, in view of this abundance of early coins, why does the sequence stop abruptly after *c*700 – why are there hardly any later Anglo-Saxon coins at all?

Did other metal finds give any sort of clue? There were about 2,000 altogether. Many were broken fragments beyond identification, but there were some 200 artefacts which, though generally damaged, were recognizable and could be dated, like the coins, to the seventh century or thereabouts. There was a range of brooches, numerous buckles and belt-fittings, studs and strap-ends, various pins, loops and fasteners from clothing, and a selection of plates and catches that might have come from wooden boxes. Most of the objects were bronze, but a small scoop, two finger-rings and some bits of scrap were gold. This is what Anglo-Saxon archaeologists call a 'productive site' – not productive in the sense that things were made there in the past (though they might have been), but productive of metal finds when detected today. So it is an archaeological definition, not an historical one, and it leaves open the question: what *were* productive sites?

There is no simple answer. One problem might be that results quickly get distorted. Once a detecting team knows a site – like Dave's field near Ipswich – is productive they keep going back to it and the haul from this one site steadily mounts. Other fields remain blanks on the map because no one is looking there. Maybe if we kept looking we would end up with productive sites everywhere. On the other hand, some productive sites had been identified even before metal-detecting took off in the mid-1970s, and there does seem to be a contrast between Anglo-Saxon sites which show up in fieldwalking as scatters of pottery without much else, and those like Dave's that are rich in coins and metalwork. Even if the distinction is valid, however, it still does not follow that sites can be divided neatly into two basic types: productive and the rest. There might be different types of productive. A royal palace, a monastery, a nobleman's estate, a 'minster' (or mother) church, an *emporium* (a trading centre), a manufacturing area: could they not all be productive of metalwork? And might not sites change – from being productive in one period to 'non-productive' in the next? Dave's field seems to be a case in point. It *is* a productive site, but *only* in the seventh century – perhaps there was a settlement there at other times, but an ordinary one.

In archaeology the detailed questions about a site can only be answered by excavation. Dave had long been keen on this, but it was not until 2003 that the money was available. Television archaeology has its advantages: the BBC wanted to shoot a programme, so they stumped up the money for a dig. There was a little tension, though, when the archaeologists came in. They did a geophysics survey of the field, but the results were unclear. The subsoil is sand, gravel and chalk, which is loose and fast draining, so you do not get the sharp contrasts, as you do with clay for example, between the fills of pits and ditches and the undisturbed ground into which they are cut. The geophysics on Dave's field revealed a lot of natural 'anomalies' – irregular areas of disturbance below the surface that are caused geologically. Sometimes, where anomalies are artificial – that is, caused by human intervention – they form regular patterns: a series of similar-sized circles for rubbish pits, a long straight line for a field boundary, neat curves or right angles for a ditched enclosure. But here, as so often, the computer printout was much less clear: a lot of blobs and squiggles that might be something, but might not. The plan, however, was to target the possible anomalies, and 12 'evaluation' trenches were laid out across the field. There was only money for a week's work by a small team, and Dave was unhappy. 'A lot of the trenches were squandered,' he said afterwards. 'If they'd listened to me, we'd have been in a much happier situation. I knew where the buildings were because of where the finds had come from and where we'd seen the black layer.'

The Black Layer

Dave had studied the area closely. He is dismissive of people who just get out their metal-detectors to see what they can find. For him, 'the whole thing has become a study – a serious study of the whole area to find out what was going on here'. Years before, Dave's detecting team had followed a plough, looking at the colour of the soil freshly turned up, and plotted an area of about 8 acres where there was a rich black layer beneath the upper plough-soil. Subsequently they had got permission to dig a small test pit – only about 3 feet across – to check that Dave's guess about the black layer was right. It was: black soil meant Anglo-Saxon occupation. Human settlement generates huge amounts of organic waste – vegetable matter, animal dung, rotted timbers, human excrement – and also a lot of burning – on hearths, in ovens, to dispose of rubbish or due to accidental fires. The decayed matter and charcoal that result darken the soil on settlement sites. So when the professionals came in, Dave was convinced he knew better than the geophysics where to put the trenches.

But archaeology is about much more than metallic finds and one black layer. 'It's no good just targeting the find-spots,' explains Linzi Everett, the field archaeologist from Suffolk County Council Archaeological Service in charge of the dig. 'We need to sample the field systematically by following up the geophysics hot spots. Otherwise we'll go home not knowing what they are. We need as full a context for the finds as we can get.' Even so, the first couple of days of the BBC dig were disappointing. The archaeologists found only a few uninteresting features that were either post-medieval, undatable or geological. Nothing Anglo-Saxon. Maybe Dave was right and the trenches were in the wrong place. Then, on the third day, they started finding what they were looking for, starting with two or three 'sunken featured buildings' (or 'SFBs' as they are known in archaeological parlance). By themselves the SFBs merely indicated 'Anglo-Saxon'. Shortly afterwards, however, they found something really impressive that confirmed beyond doubt that they were on the site of a high-status Anglo-Saxon settlement.

Anglo-Saxon Huts and Halls

SFBs are found on all early and many later Anglo-Saxon domestic sites. They are so-called because their most obvious characteristic is that they have a shallow dug-out hollow that is roughly rectangular in shape and usually measures about 6½ feet by 10 (though they can range in size from 5 feet on the short width to 30 feet on the long one). Around the edge there are usually a variable number of substantial post holes, showing that a roofed timber structure covered the hollow. Was the hollow an underground cellar with a timber floor across the top, or did you step down into the lowered surface when you entered the hut? Very occasionally there is some

Right: A reconstructed 'SFB' or 'sunken featured building' at West Stow in Suffolk.

Above: An Anglo-Saxon 'hall' at West Stow, reconstructed using techniques available at the time the original was

evidence, but usually we do not know. At the reconstructed Anglo-Saxon village at West Stow in Suffolk – built on the site of an original village where 7 halls and 69 SFBs were excavated by Stanley West from 1965 to 1972 – archaeologists have created full-size versions of both possibilities. What is clear, though, is that SFBs were subordinate structures. They were relatively small, and there is evidence from West Stow and elsewhere that they could be used for ancillary activities like weaving and storage. Especially instructive was SFB 15 at West Stow, which had been destroyed by fire. Excavators found carbonized wooden floor-boards at the base of the hollow, overlain by neatly arranged clay loom-weights, these in turn overlain by further wooden boards, presumably as a result of the collapse of the walls. There was even a thin layer of silty sand at the very bottom of the hollow, as if fine-grained material had seeped through the floorboards above when the building was in use. Rarely is the evidence for timbered floors so good, but the invariably subordinate character of SFBs is proved by the presence alongside them of much more substantial structures: large timber houses or 'halls'.

You need quite a bit of imagination to be a good archaeologist. Long-vanished buildings can leave but the slightest trace. Linzi's highest trenches were about two-thirds of the way up the field from the valley bottom. The soil was thinner here, the archaeology closer to the surface, and as the digger pulled back the plough-soil and revealed the underlying sand, a dark line appeared, less than 2 feet wide. Then there was a 'return': the line turned a right angle and carried on. Soon they had the other end, a second return, showing three sides of a possible box. It measured 35 feet in length. When the trench was extended laterally, they found the fourth side and got the crossways dimension too: 23 feet. It was a building. A large, rectangular, Anglo-Saxon timber hall – now reduced to a line in the sand. Not only was it a good size, it had been built using the 'post-in-trench' method. Instead of a series of individual post holes – the usual and easier method in the seventh century – a continuous trench had been dug so that the timber uprights could be more carefully aligned with one another and with other elements of the construction like the planks or wattle-hurdles that formed the walls. Here is where you need that archaeological imagination. A continuous line in the sand instead of a series of blobs means a timber-framed building where all the parts fitted tightly together. In seventh-century Anglo-Saxon England, a post-in-trench hall meant you were top drawer.

There was something else from the excavation that pointed in the same direction: in a trench further down the slope there was the vitrified lining of a hearth, indicating high temperatures and possible industrial use. This tied in with detailed analysis of Dave's collection of metalwork. The finds included a handful of unfinished artefacts, several bits of bronze scrap, fragments of gold jewellery from which garnets had been prized out, and one or two gold coins with evidence of filing, cutting or partial melting. John Newman, a senior figure in the Suffolk archaeology unit and a leading Anglo-Saxon specialist, was in no doubt as to how to interpret this:

> On high-status sites, you get the metalworking. The material is rare, so craft-workers are attached to great houses, to patrons with access to bronze, silver and gold. It's important to remember the evidence is often slight. Anglo-Saxon metalworking was basically low-tech – it was the person's skills that were crucial – and any waste material was too valuable not to be carefully collected up. The evidence we've got points to a lot of metalworking on this site, perhaps including coin minting, though we have no direct evidence for this. This fits with the post-in-trench construction for the hall. I imagine this to have been a sprawling aristocratic settlement with a complex of halls in the centre, and the SFBs on the outskirts, where the metalworking and other crafts were happening.

An Anglo-Saxon Cemetery

There was one final clue to the importance of the people who had lived on Dave's field in the seventh century. About half a mile away, at the top of the facing slope on the other side of the valley, there was a cemetery. Although part of it was lost to quarrying, some

53 inhumation graves (in which the whole body is buried) were excavated late in 1999. They were all, judging by the type of grave-goods, seventh or early eighth century in date – what archaeologists call a 'final phase' cemetery. When the Anglo-Saxons first arrived in south-eastern Britain, mainly at various times in the fifth century, they were pagans who buried their dead with grave-goods to accompany them on the journey to Valhalla. This is crucial to Early Anglo-Saxon archaeology. Only a handful of settlement sites of this period have been excavated, compared with some 1,500 cemeteries, either in whole or in part, which have yielded evidence of not fewer than 30,000 burials. Early Anglo-Saxon archaeology is basically an archaeology of the dead. Spong Hill in Norfolk, for example, contained 57 inhumation graves and some 2,500 cremations in funerary urns, all dating from the late fifth to the late sixth century. Some men had been buried with spears and shields, and many women with brooches and beads. Sites of this kind are relatively easy to find and rewarding to excavate – unlike settlements. The huge numbers

Below: Miranda Krestovnikoff with experimental archaeologist, Richard Darrah, who is reconstructing the bed burial from minimal evidence uncovered during the dig.

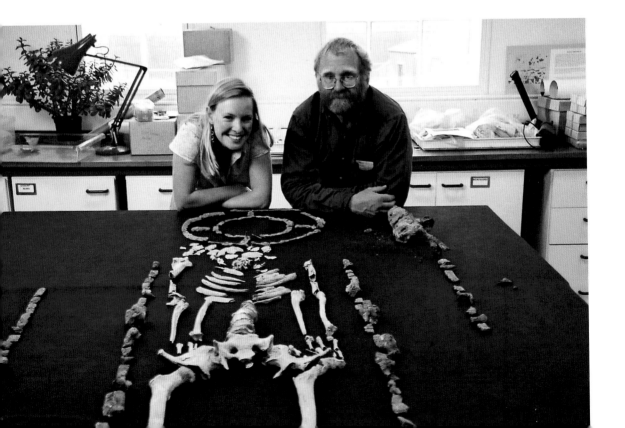

of artefacts recovered enable specialists to organize the material into chronological sequences. Each period has its distinctive 'assemblage': a mixture of artefact types – certain styles of beads, brooches, belt-fittings, decorative motifs on pottery, and so on – that tend to be found together. The Christian conversion changed things radically. During the seventh century the new religion altered funerary rites for ever and emptied burials of their grave-goods. The conversion took time, however – two or three generations – some people hedged their bets, and the process of transition gave rise to 'final phase' assemblages. The dead were no longer cremated and bodies would usually be aligned west–east – in conformity with Christian practice – but they often still had grave-goods, sometimes including pagan images.

The cemetery excavated opposite Dave's field had been confidently dated to the seventh century – the period of Christian conversion. What had also been clear was that the cemetery was highly stratified – and a growing gap between the top and the bottom of Anglo-Saxon society was another feature of the seventh century generally. A handful of the graves had been rich. Four burials had ring-ditches around them and probably mounds over the top, and among the better quality grave-goods there were coins, weapons, and bronze bowls in Merovingian style, perhaps from northern France. There was also one burial in a super-rich class of its own. An Anglo-Saxon woman had been buried outstretched on her iron bed. Now beds were luxury items – most people probably slept on the ground or at best on wooden boards. Here was someone not only rich enough to own a bed, but whose family could afford to bury her with it. Only a few other Anglo-Saxon bed burials are known. So, while a majority of the excavated burials in the cemetery contained very little in the way of grave-goods, the minority that did seemed to represent a series of ranks extending up towards the very top of seventh-century society. What sort of people would the top ones have been? Who might have lived in the 'complex of halls' across the valley? To find the answers, we need to look further afield – but not all that far, for the Ipswich area has the richest seventh-century archaeology in Britain. This was where, 1,400 years ago, a new politics of English kingship was being forged.

The Sutton Hoo Ship Burial

Early in 1938, Mrs Edith Pretty, the owner of the Sutton Hoo estate – 400 acres of sandy heath and woodland on the Deben estuary a few miles north-east of Ipswich – was casting

Above: A masterpiece of excavation reveals an entire Anglo-Saxon ship represented by lines of rusty rivets and stains in the sand. Right: An artist's reconstruction of the great Mound 1 burial, showing the ship as it might have been.

around for an archaeologist. She could see from her window, several hundred yards away, a group of low grassy mounds that looked interesting. They lay on the edge of a 100-foot-high bluff immediately overlooking the river: a very prominent location. The curator of the Ipswich Museum suggested Basil Brown, a local man who was the museum's archaeologist, and Mrs Pretty duly hired him, gave him lodgings in the chauffeur's cottage and assigned him two of the estate labourers as assistants. Results that first summer were mixed. Trenches were cut across three mounds, and it was clear that they had, as suspected, covered burials. However, each had been robbed, its burial disturbed, and any grave-goods either taken or damaged.

Brown had nevertheless established three things of importance. First, from the fragments of artefacts recovered, he knew the burials had been Anglo-Saxon. Second, from those same fragments, he could tell that the burials had been rich. Third and, as it was to turn out, most important, while excavating Mound 2 he had correctly guessed the identity and significance of a series of rusty iron lumps found buried within it. Each one was a few inches long and had a domed head at one end and a squarish plate at the other. They were rivets which had once secured the planks of a wooden ship – and some of them had been found *in situ*, at the base of the cutting, which was 'boat-shaped without any question'. The burial

chamber had been robbed out, and the excavation techniques of 1938 had made a further hash of it, but it was apparent that Mound 2 had covered an Anglo-Saxon ship-burial.

The following summer, Mrs Pretty suggested to Brown that he tackle Mound 1, the largest in the group. On the fourth day of the new season one of the labourers called out, 'Here's a bit of iron', and held up a rivet. Brown stopped the work to investigate the find-spot himself. Trowelling away the sand in the vicinity, he quickly uncovered five more rivets – in a line, regularly spaced; that is, *in situ*. Brown's moment of genius was now at hand. To understand his breakthrough, we have to step back from Mound 1 and recall how all digs were done in the 1930s. No one – that is, no one – excavated using what we would now call an 'open area' method. All excavation involved digging trenches through a site, recording the layers in the vertical sides of those trenches (or 'sections'), and hoping that the trenches were in the right place to hit the important archaeology at the bottom. In the case of burial mounds, you drove a trench through the middle and hoped to hit the burial itself at the centre point. Or worse, you simply dug straight down from the top of the mound.

Brown now knew that Mound 1, like Mound 2, contained a ship. Neither a central pit nor a crossways trench could reveal that ship. So he invented a new way of digging a mound. They would gradually remove all the soil overlying the rivets, but the rivets themselves – and the dark stains that were all that was left of the planks they had secured – would be left *in situ*, so that the excavators would end up, in effect, inside the hull of the ship. It was one of the most brilliant pieces of excavation ever undertaken. At the end of it, the interior shape of an entire Anglo-Saxon ship, formed of walls of sand and parallel lines of rusty iron rivets, stood revealed. Brown was indeed, as the poet Seamus Heaney recently described him, 'the shipwright of the earth-ship'.

But there was more. The ship was huge. Built of overlapping planks fixed to a series of curving cross-beams, it was nearly 90 feet long and, at its widest point, 14 feet across. This makes it the largest ship of early Dark Age date known to us. Not only does it represent a grave offering of enormous value, its position in a burial mound at the top of the 100-foot-high bluff represents an enormous investment of labour during the funerary rite. The realization, therefore, that the burial chamber, a dark rectangle amidships, was intact – that the medieval tomb-robbers had failed to find it – was awesome. What would it contain? What would have been considered fitting to accompany this great ship-lord to Valhalla? Mrs Pretty, alerted to the importance of the Mound 1 discoveries by visiting luminaries, allowed the British Museum and the Office of Works to appoint the Cambridge don Charles Phillips to oversee further work on the site. So it was that in July and August 1939, as the Second World War approached, Phillips, with Brown as his assistant, and a small group of archaeological friends, excavated what turned out to be the most richly furnished burial chamber ever discovered in Britain.

Grave-goods symbolize earthly role and rank. They are there so that a man will be recognized for who he is when he reaches Valhalla, and be offered a place proper to his station in the great mead-hall of the gods. For archaeologists, they are a gift of knowledge from the past, and there is none greater than the assemblage from the Sutton Hoo ship-burial. The famous helmet with its tinned-bronze relief panels, the shield decorated with golden ornaments, the sword with gold and garnet hilt, and the coat of chain mail: these tell us he was a warrior. A bronze 'Coptic' bowl, the huge silver 'Anastasius Dish', a set of silver bowls, and two silver spoons – all objects from the Byzantine Empire – reveal a man of taste, well connected, with Mediterranean sophistication. His drinking horns, bottles and cups, his gaming pieces and the lyre, his three bronze, Celtic hanging-bowls, his buckets and cauldrons: all of these speak of feasting and drinking in the mead-hall. The whetstone sceptre with its bronze stag, the gold and garnet shoulder-clasps, the great gold buckle, the beautifully decorated belt and strap fittings, the leather purse containing 37 gold *tremisses*, each from a different mint in Merovingian Gaul: when they saw him arrayed in all this regalia, could the gods have been in any doubt that this man was a king?

Below: A 'sand man' from Sutton Hoo. Only later were techniques developed for the recovery of these bodies, often formed of nothing but crusty, discoloured sand.

The Missing King

No body was ever found at Sutton Hoo. Almost certainly this was because its recovery was beyond the techniques known to Phillips's team. They reported finding crusty brown lumps in the sand – to which they attached no significance. All bone and flesh would have been destroyed by the highly acidic sand of Sutton Hoo – the area is naturally a rough heathland. It was not until Martin Carver's new excavations in 1986–92 that a technique was developed for the recovery of the 'sand people' interred there, as Carver explains:

> The first thing to appear was a crusty brown lump of sand, the consistency of sugar, which persevered under the trowel and curved away downwards. This was a part of the decayed body itself. Follow the edges of the surface of the brown crust, taking away the softer fill beside it, and the shape would be revealed: a head, an arm, a pelvis, a leg. The whole sand body was eventually revealed, not a skeleton but a brown person. Bone would sometimes survive, but it would be inside the crusty sand jacket, showing that what was being defined was the shape of the flesh itself.

So the king under Mound 1 had almost certainly been there – until the crusty brown lumps that were all that remained of him dissolved under the trowel. He had been buried in the bowels of a great ship surrounded by a glittering array of precious and finely crafted grave-goods. Who was he? We can never be sure, but we can have a good guess. The latest of the 37 Merovingian gold coins in his purse dated to the 620s. Though some grave-goods were much earlier – the Anastasius Dish, for example, whose Byzantine silverware control stamps date its manufacture between 491 and 518 – these are items of great value which are likely to have been treasured and passed on over many generations. Many of the later pieces, however, can be dated on stylistic grounds to the late sixth or early seventh century. So the coin date is confirmed. Then there is the 'iconography': the artistic images and motifs decorating the objects. Sometimes we seem to see the warriors and beasts of pagan Germanic myth, but the silver bowls are decorated with Christian crosses, and the two spoons, possibly a christening gift, are inscribed *PAULOS* and *SAULOS*. Most telling, however, is that among the many distant connections evident in the grave-goods assemblage there is a link with southern Sweden. The helmet and the shield especially were probably, in the words of the official Mound 1 excavation report, 'made in Sweden or by armourers from Sweden working in Suffolk exclusively in their traditional Swedish manner and with Swedish dies, moulds and other equipment'. We know too that in Sweden during the Dark Ages they buried people in ships and heaped mounds over them.

The early seventh-century date, the 'final phase' pagan–Christian ambiguity, the Swedishness of ship-burial and of some of the grave-goods: all the evidence supports – and none other contradicts – an identification of the Mound 1 man as Raedwald, lord of the Wuffings, king of East Anglia, and *bretwalda* (overking) of all the English. Our main historical source for him is the Venerable Bede's *History of the English Church and People*.

The Venerable Bede

Bede (*c*673–735) was an Anglo-Saxon monk who lived in a monastery at Jarrow in Northumbria and completed his great work of history in *c*731. Most of what we know about the first Anglo-Saxon kingdoms we owe to him. Starting with the Roman Conquest, he gives a summary history of Britain up until the mission of St Augustine in 597, when the conversion of the Anglo-Saxons began. From then until his own time, he provides a far more detailed – though often one-sided – account of the work of Anglo-Saxon kings, missionaries and bishops. Without Bede, we would not know even the names of most of the movers and shakers of seventh-century England.

The Wuffings were probably the descendants of invaders from Sweden who arrived in East Anglia around 500. There is much debate still about what such 'invasions' were like. The Anglo-Saxon migrations lasted a century or so, but did they involve hundreds of thousands and wholesale 'ethnic cleansing' of the native British population? Or was it only tens of thousands, with most new settlements on virgin land, and peaceful coexistence with neighbouring Britons? Or was it fewer still, perhaps no more than several thousand altogether, but forming powerful bands of warrior nobles able to establish themselves as a new ruling class, much as the Normans would do half a millennium later? No evidence is conclusive one way or another. The material culture of eastern Britain quickly became overwhelmingly Germanic, and the Celtic language was displaced by the Anglo-Saxon tongue from which modern English has evolved. However, there are many cases where 'élite domination' alone, without mass migration, has transformed popular culture. Most of Scotland, Ireland and Wales were never settled by large numbers of English; yet the Celtic

Right: This artist's impression shows Raedwald, King of East Anglia in the early seventh century, wearing some of the rich artefacts found in the chamber in the bottom of the ship excavated at Sutton Hoo.

languages had almost died out there by the mid twentieth century. Early Anglo-Saxon society was certainly stratified. Ancient law-codes make distinctions between Anglo-Saxons and Britons, between freemen, half-free and slaves, and between different ranks within each. Early cemeteries seem to reflect this. At Spong Hill, one of the most elaborate graves had been covered by an earth mound and contained a man buried with spear, shield, sword and bucket. Nearby were the graves of men with spears and shields. Was this an Anglo-Saxon lord and his retainers? The majority of graves were much simpler. Did they contain the subject Britons who had worked the land for Anglo-Saxon masters?

Whatever the numbers of Anglo-Saxon migrants in the fifth century, and whatever their relationship with the British inhabitants, the hierarchy of rank in this new society became more extended during the following century. Some raised themselves up from the mass of warrior chiefs and became kings. A man called Wehha was 'the first to rule over the East Angles in Britain', probably around 550, and he was followed by his son, Wuffa, who gave his name to the royal line, then by his grandson, Tyttla, and finally, in 599, by his great-grandson, Raedwald. Or so we are led to believe.

The Cemetery at Sutton Hoo

The problem with Anglo-Saxon royal lineages is that they were written down much later, when established kings sought legitimacy through claims of long descent. Both Caesar and Woden appear among the dynastic founders claimed by Anglo-Saxon royalty. It is probably true to say that kings appear earlier in Anglo-Saxon texts than they did in Anglo-Saxon reality. John Newman got the chance to test the archaeology behind the propaganda at Sutton Hoo itself in the summer of 2000.

The National Trust were planning a new visitor and exhibition centre with extensive car and coach parking (the complex is now open). A rescue dig was essential in advance of development. The new site lay a few hundred yards north of the royal cemetery, and, as it happened, some 15 years before a local farmer

Left: A gilt-bronze dragon with a jewelled eye and bared teeth: one of several stunning shield decorations from the Mound 1 burial at Sutton Hoo.

harrowing a field had brought up a spectacular find very close by. It comprised three pieces of a shallow brass bucket about the size of a casserole dish. The base was missing and only half the handle was found, but the overall preservation was good, and it could be seen that the vessel was decorated. There was an inscription in bad Greek around the top, and beneath it a frieze of hunters and their prey executed with punches and chisels on the hammered metal. The Bromeswell Bucket – as it came to be known – was a rare find. Only a handful like it are known, and almost certainly they were all made at some point during the sixth century in the same workshop in Antioch. By what mechanism did a Byzantine bucket end up in a field in Suffolk? John Newman's diggers set out to find the answer.

Over several weeks, they exposed a large part of an Anglo-Saxon cemetery containing 19 inhumations and 17 cremations, some of them clustered round an old Bronze Age barrow. This much was pretty routine. What was unusual was the proportion of burials that were elaborate and richly furnished, and the overall quality of the grave-goods recovered. Nine of the cremations were enclosed by small ring-ditches. One had been placed in a Celtic hanging-bowl with beautifully decorated ring-attachments ('escutcheons'), and four lesser cremations clustered around it, each with a broken fragment of bronze vessel, perhaps symbolic in some way of the unity of the four and their possible leader. Among the inhumations, 13 male graves contained typical Anglo-Saxon weapon sets of spear and shield, but two also had swords (a much more expensive item of equipment). The proportion of warriors was exceptionally high. So was the quality of their gear. One of the warrior burials contained a lavish wooden shield covered in leather and decorated with bronze and silvered attachments, including a gilt-bronze disc on the apex of the iron boss, eight gilded studs, and stylized images of a sea creature and a bird of prey. According to Angela Evans of the British Museum, 'The quality of metalwork is extraordinary – exceptionally well made, beautiful and well designed. These objects are among the best of their type. Put them alongside the other weapons, the Celtic hanging-bowl, and the Bromeswell Bucket, and we seem to be dealing with an upwardly mobile community.'

At the end of the dig, John Newman was in no doubt about the significance of the new discoveries:

> Sutton Hoo has always appeared a bit isolated. Why was it here? Anglo-Saxon kingship seemed to appear out of nowhere. It makes much more sense that we now have a whole funerary landscape. The northern cemetery begins around 525–50 and probably overlaps with the southern one. At this earlier date, we've got burials showing clear signs of social status, growing differentiation and very rich finds overall for a sixth-century Anglo-Saxon cemetery.

Above: Top Suffolk archaeologist John Newman explains things to Miranda Krestovnikoff.

Perhaps the warrior with the fancy shield was one of Raedwald's ancestors. Perhaps the Bromeswell Bucket was a Wuffing heirloom. Were the first kings of East Anglia buried at Sutton Hoo because this was their ancestral seat? And were they, in the mid sixth century, on the last leg of a rise to power that had transformed them into kings by the early seventh?

Sutton Hoo is not the only site in the Ipswich area with things to tell us about the origins of English kingship. The rivers of south-east Suffolk – the Deben, the Orwell, the Stour – are obvious points of entry for invaders from the North Sea, and there is a thick cluster of Early Anglo-Saxon cemeteries around the estuaries. Nor was Sutton Hoo the only later cemetery with mounded ship-burials. Another existed a short distance away at Snape Common. It was investigated by antiquarians in 1827 and 1862. In one of the mounds they found a ship at least 46 feet long, and, although the burial chamber had been robbed, remaining grave-goods included two iron spearheads, a glass 'claw-beaker' and a gold finger-ring.

Then there is Ipswich itself, which became a major wic or *emporium* (a long-distance trade port) in the mid seventh century. There was nothing inevitable about this: seventh-century ports were not natural outgrowths of expanding commerce. Trade was controlled. Markets were regulated. You had to get permission to operate, and anyway you needed protection. So merchants and goods were 'embedded' in the local power structure, and ports emerged where there was a powerful authority promoting them. The rise of Ipswich – eventually to cover 125 acres and rank among the biggest towns in Anglo-Saxon England – was almost certainly linked with the ascendancy of the Wuffing dynasty. Its trade was mainly with the Rhineland, from which pottery, wine, glass and quern-stones were imported, while local workshops produced pottery and goods in leather, bone and bronze. Many of the rich objects in the Sutton Hoo treasure undoubtedly passed through Ipswich. And what of a royal residence? None has yet been found, although Bede mentions Rendlesham, a short distance upriver from Sutton Hoo. Probably, though, there would have been more than one. Early Anglo-Saxon kings owned numerous scattered estates, and they and their courts were peripatetic, constantly on the move across their kingdoms – hearing petitions, settling disputes, dispensing justice, imposing order, trying to make a reality of their shaky claim to power.

A Northern Palace

What would seventh-century Rendlesham – or any other East Anglian royal estate-centre – have been like? There is another seventh-century royal palace mentioned by Bede that, unlike Rendlesham, has been excavated. It lies near the furthest limit of Anglo-Saxon power, some 40 miles north of Hadrian's Wall, in an area of cold and desolate hill-country. Yeavering palace was one of the seats of the kings of Northumbria, and Bede tells us that in 627 the missionary Paulinus stayed there with King Edwin (616–32), 'and remained 36 days constantly occupied in instructing and baptising'. The site was abandoned shortly afterwards and was soon lost to memory. It suddenly reappeared in 1949. An astonishing aerial photograph revealed a set of large rectangular timber buildings in the form of dark lines (where crops were growing strongly in the buried wall-trenches) against a pale, blotchy background. During the 1950s and early 1960s, under Brian Hope-Taylor, it became the focus of what Philip Rahtz described as 'perhaps the finest excavation that has ever taken place in this country'. Rahtz was a contemporary, no mean excavator himself, and had also, as it happens, tackled an Anglo-Saxon royal palace (at Cheddar in Somerset). This was praise indeed. He continued:

> Hope-Taylor, working under conditions of considerable difficulty, worked out construction and destruction sequences in soil in which the fillings of the foundation trenches were described by him as 'a yellow-buff colour in a buff-yellow subsoil', a distinction which disappeared in dry weather! In spite of this, we have the plan of some 20 buildings …

Among the most important were a succession of halls, the finest of which, from the dating evidence, was probably that of King Edwin himself or his immediate predecessor, King Aethelfrith (592–616). It was more than 80 feet long and nearly 40 wide, and the walls were built of planks over 5 inches thick set into deep trenches. There are many surviving examples of medieval timber buildings on this scale – tithe barns, guildhalls, grand houses in both town and country. The massiveness of the timbers, the complexity of the structure, the sophistication of the carpentry: these are the things about them that impress. Sometimes, too, we see

Above: This artist's reconstruction shows the monumental seventh-century royal palace at Yeavering in Northumberland.

elaborate wood-carving. This is an art form of which only the shadow survives from Anglo-Saxon times, but we can guess how much there must have been, and of what quality. The art that survives on stone and metal has the chip-carved form of work on wood. The art of the wood-sculptor was the model for the rest. Imagine Yeavering palace, then, adorned with horned gods, mythic beasts and dragon's heads in a maze of interlace. Imagine it like King Hrothgar's in *Beowulf*: 'a wonder of the world … a hall of halls … towering with gables wide and high'. That is the meaning of those yellow-buff lines in the buff-yellow soil that disappeared in the sun.

Left: A page from the late seventh-century Anglo-Saxon epic, Beowulf. *Here, King Hrothgar of the Danes commands his men 'to make a hall-building, a mead-hall greater than any ever heard of by the children of men … '*

Anglo-Saxon Kingship

The hall Linzi Everett found on Dave Cummings's field near Ipswich was barely a quarter the size of Edwin's palace at Yeavering. Nonetheless, it was a good size for an Anglo-Saxon hall, and taken all in all, considering the gold ring, the early coins, the metalworking debris, the bed burial on the opposite hill, we have a site of very high status close to the centre of the new kingdom of East Anglia. It could have been a royal estate-centre. Linzi's hall may not even be the main one. There were subsidiary halls at Yeavering no bigger than this. Perhaps there is still a king's hall buried somewhere in Dave's field. There are other possibilities, too, and in considering these we must delve deeper into the character of early kingship. Consider these salutary comments by the Oxford historian James Campbell:

Of six East Anglian kings in less than 40 years, five died violently … One of the great differences between medieval and Dark Age kings is that while the former were rarely killed in battle (a king's ransom was worth far too much for that), the latter often were, for it seems to have been normal to kill kings and nobles if they were captured … A king, no matter how great, was quite likely to end as Oswald of Northumbria did in 642, with his head and hands stuck up on stakes on the battlefield. There were threats within as well as without. Neither in East Anglia, nor in any other kingdom, was there a settled system of succession. It seems that any male member of the royal family, widely defined, could succeed if he could get the required support and acceptance. ... Such circumstances were among those which generated feud ...

It was, then, an unstable world, where borders were fluid and dynastic claims contested. England was filling up with would-be kings and would-be states. War would decide which endured. And war needed armies. Anglo-Saxon kingship was essentially a struggle for the land, tribute and men on which success in war depended. The *Tribal Hidage*, a document dating from probably the seventh or eighth century, seems to be a tribute list for the kingdom of Mercia (in the Midlands), specifying the number of 'hides' at which each subject community was assessed. A hide was a unit of land 'sufficient to support one family', so that from a community's total 'hidage' royal officials could estimate the amount of tribute owed to the king (usually in the form of food-renders), the days of labour-service due on public works (like frontier defences), and the number of men required for the militia (known as the *fyrd*) in wartime. The one or two scraps of evidence we have indicate that it was roughly one soldier for every five hides.

How on earth was this made to work? There were no metalled roads. Very few people could read and write. The royal government employed only a handful of clerks. Central to the state-building ambitions of early Anglo-Saxon kings was the subordination of the existing nobility to royal authority. The sorts of men who had been buried with swords in the sixth century – local chiefs, tribal leaders, the people who had given their names to Anglo-Saxon villages – had to become, in the seventh, the officials and knights of the king. There is an old idea that Anglo-Saxon society was democratic – that it was governed by popular assemblies or 'folk-moots' meeting on local village greens. This is contrasted with the oppressiveness of Norman rule after 1066. It is a romantic myth. Anglo-Saxon England was a highly structured class society. When kings emerged, they formed the peaks of pyramids of ranks, without which they could not have remained in power. To survive, they had both to centralize decision-making power in their own hands, and to create an administration able to transmit commands to all parts of the kingdom. The Laws of King Ine of Wessex (*c*690) refer to *ealdormen* (later 'earls') as royal officials each of whom was in charge of an administrative district. Many were probably kinsmen of the king, but in the long run loyalty depended on reward, and these top nobles were provided with estates and became like feudal barons. In Middle Anglo-Saxon times (c650–850), the land was probably divided into great estates, usually centred on an expanse of especially fertile land. Sometimes a faint imprint of such estates survives in the landscape: the overall lie of the land, natural boundaries like rivers, the shape of later parishes. Telltale signs are often found in the place names of both parishes and settlements. Primary settlements often had names ending in -ing and/or -ham, as in Birmingham, which means 'village of Beorma's tribe'. These settlements often lie in large central parishes, in contrast to the later, secondary settlements in the smaller parishes round about, with names implying they were originally offshoots (for example, ending in -ton, meaning 'settlement or farm') or marginal (like those ending in -ley, meaning 'woodland clearing'). As new land was colonized, as populations grew and lordships multiplied, the great estates of Middle Anglo-Saxon England were broken up, creating the more complex pattern of estates and parishes recorded by the Domesday Book in 1086. The imprint left by these great estates reveals something of how the land was originally parcelled out to the king's relatives and officials – the *ealdormen* of the law-codes.

The Church was also a beneficiary of royal patronage. Before his accession, Raedwald had spent time at the court of King Aethelbert of Kent, who had married a Frankish Christian called Bertha and then invited St Augustine's mission to Canterbury in 597. Raedwald wobbled. Back home, according to Bede, 'he had in the same temple an altar for the holy sacrifice of Christ side-by-side with an altar on which victims were offered to the devil'. The grave-goods in Mound 1 confirm the ambivalence. Matters remained unclear for some time after Raedwald's death – his son and successor Eorpwald converted, but was immediately killed by a pagan rival – and it was not until the reign of King Sigbert that the conversion of the East Anglian court became irrevocable. Monks arrived from Ireland and Gaul in the 630s. Land was granted them to build monasteries on the coast. One monk named Felix became the first bishop of East Anglia. Missionaries fanned out across the hinterland. King Sigbert retired to a monastery to devote himself 'to winning an everlasting kingdom'. In the succeeding decades, the Church became a great power in East Anglian society, receiving lands from the king, enjoying the patronage of local nobility, and building for itself a network of 'minster' churches and consecrated burial grounds that acted as centres for groups of priests servicing the surrounding villages. East Anglia was caught up in a tide of Christian conversion that swept across Anglo-Saxon England in the first half of the seventh century.

The timing was no coincidence. Kings and bishops arose together. The paganism of tribal communities was overwhelmed by state-backed Christianity. The great medieval alliance of Church and state was forged in the seventh century. The advantages of this alliance to the early Anglo-Saxon kings were considerable. The Church was a highly centralized body able to promote conformity and loyalty in a world where politics and religion were inseparable. In building royal states, it was important to convince men that god and the king were in harmony. The Church also had the organization and skills to deliver. In the kingdom of the illiterate, the man who can write may not actually rule, but he can certainly make himself very useful to those who do. It is not an accident that the Latin word *clericus* gives us both 'clerk' and 'clergyman'. *Styli* – implements for writing on wax tablets – are fairly common Anglo-Saxon finds from the seventh century onwards. Dave Cummings has found two on his site. There is much debate about what they signify. A monastery? A church? More probably it is any sort of high-status site, all of which are likely to have had priest-clerks on their staff.

Not least among the Church's attractions was its aura of *Romanitas*. The Roman Empire had become Christian in the fourth century, and when the western provinces fell in the fifth, it was very often the local churches alone that survived as enclaves of Roman culture. Early Dark Age Christianity became associated with 'civilized' urban life, with Latin literacy and classical learning, with the values and traditions of Old Rome. New kings for a new age needed models from the past. What did it mean to be a king? How should kings act? What was needed to make others obey? The best models available were Roman ones. We can see it at Sutton Hoo. 'The graves can be read like literature in pre-literate culture,' argues Martin Carver, who led the excavations there in 1986–92. 'There are statements about rank, status, culture, power and so on. The Anglo-Saxon world around 600 was changing. Small lordships were coalescing into a kingdom. It was a highly stressful time, full of uncertainties. Who are we? What do we believe? Who are our friends? Sutton Hoo is a theatre for displaying the answers.' According to Helen Geake, another leading Anglo-Saxon specialist, one answer in particular stands out: 'If you look at what they're buried with, these early Anglo-Saxon kings seem to have been dressing up as Romans – claiming a right to rule as the spiritual descendants of the Roman emperors.' When seventh-century Anglo-Saxon kings became patrons of the Church, they were hiring the top firm of spin doctors and a highly effective PR 'concept'.

So we can sketch out the form of an early Anglo-Saxon kingdom. The king was peripatetic, moving around his kingdom with a courtly retinue, stopping for a month at one royal residence, for two or three at another. The retinue was supported by food-renders levied on the peasants of each estate. Other land, also organized in great estates, was parcelled out to an aristocracy of district-officers, the *ealdormen*, or to the Church, which provided the seventh-century world with its bureaucrats and propagandists. This infrastructure of government ensured the flows of tribute, labour-service and military manpower on which the whole edifice rested. Though we cannot know whether it was royal, aristocratic or even ecclesiastical, it is a fair guess that Dave's site was an estate-centre in the seventh century. Perhaps Raedwald himself stayed here. Perhaps one of his kinsmen owned it. Certainly there will have been people here who knew Raedwald personally: people of rank who shared his mead-hall.

Below: The gold fittings from the Anglo-Saxon sword handle found beside a small river in North Lincolnshire.

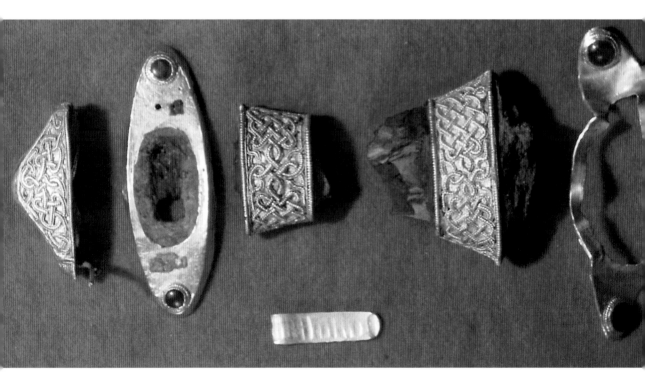

The Sword by the River

How did kings maintain their position among the warrior lords of seventh-century England? What bonds of allegiance bound together the men who shared a mead-hall? What code of honour united them in the service of their lord? Let us start the enquiry with another spectacular find from the seventh century that has just come to light.

Kevin Leahy, the leading archaeologist in North Lincolnshire, first got news of it when he received a phone call at the museum where he works in Scunthorpe. It was from a landowner who had recently granted permission to a local metal-detectorist to search on his land. The detectorist had found something that they both thought Kevin should see. When they brought it in, Kevin watched as they carefully unwrapped a package, revealing first one, then another, and eventually five separate pieces of Anglo-Saxon goldwork. Kevin knew it was Anglo-Saxon from the first piece – indeed, more precisely, he knew it was seventh century. He had been in Lincolnshire archaeology for 30 years, and he was now an Anglo-Saxon specialist. 'I started as a prehistorian,' he recalls wistfully, 'but I got ambushed by the Anglo-Saxons as soon as I arrived. There was a bag of their pottery on my desk the day I started at the museum, and they've been waiting for me at every turn ever since. So I know what Anglo-Saxon looks like!' So much so that he has just completed a new book on Anglo-Saxon crafts.

Above: Kevin Leahy, leading archaeologist in North Lincolnshire, on site for a Hidden Treasure *dig.*

Kevin may have been an old hand, quick to recognize seventh-century work from the style of decoration, but he was stunned to see five, separate, beautifully decorated gold pieces all from the same object. 'Normally you are thrilled to see just one piece, generally made from base metal. Rarely do you see craftsmanship like this.' They were fittings from a sword handle – a pommel cap, two plates from the pommel and crosspiece, and two gold ferrules from the hilt itself. Each bore decoration in gold filigree, the applied wire fused with the metal beneath to form an invisible bond. Garnets had been inset – 'cabochon' style, which means they had not been cut but left as pebbles and polished. The bottoms of the cells in which the garnets had been placed were formed of corrugated gold foil, which reflected the light, making them glitter. 'It was work to a very high standard. You see it occasionally if you have lots of finds passing through your hands. But not often. This was an artefact of the top aristocratic class from which kings were chosen.'

The sword fragments had been found on the edge of a field beside a small river. The river now had steep banks and was about 12 feet wide and 2 feet deep, but it had been canalized, and in Anglo-Saxon times it might have been broader and shallower, with marshes alongside. What was the sword doing here? Where was the rest of it? Was it part of a burial which included other weapons? Kevin wanted to find out and a team was sent in to investigate. There was a geophysical survey of the field, a trench was put in at the actual find-spot and the river bed was metal-detected. Nothing, however, was found – except proof that the sword handle had been disturbed very recently. The excavation showed that the deposit *beneath* that in which the finder had detected the five gold fragments contained a mid-twentieth-century light-bulb fitting! The river had been dredged and the fragments had been in the up-cast sand and gravel dumped on the bank. Perhaps the rusted blade had been destroyed then. If not, if it was still in the river bed, the metal-detector never found it, nor anything else that might have been with it.

The five fragments of gem-encrusted golden sword-hilt were left floating in an archaeological vacuum. There were as many possibilities as one could think of, and they could not be narrowed down because there was no other evidence. Maybe it was lost in battle: contested river-crossings are recorded in Anglo-Saxon histories. Maybe it was an accidental loss: even something as valuable as a gold-hilted sword might never have been recovered from a marsh. Or could its loss have been deliberate, a ritual offering to the deity of the river in those twilight years of Germanic paganism? British rivers have a habit of turning up weaponry – Bronze Age, Iron Age, sometimes Roman, occasionally Anglo-Saxon,

certainly Viking. The nearby Witham is full of it. Or could it have come from a burial? The site lies at a point where a number of parish boundaries meet. Was a warrior buried here so that he could continue to guard in death land he had once defended in life? If so, it is surprising that nothing more was found. Any warrior buried with a sword would have had other arms also – a spear, a shield, perhaps a helmet, very occasionally a coat of mail.

It is difficult to convey what a sword meant to an Anglo-Saxon. Most men probably did not fight at all: they were simply ploughmen and shepherds. The mass of men who did – the free Saxons of the *fyrd* – were armed with spear and shield. In battle, formed up shoulder to shoulder, many ranks deep, they presented to the enemy a shield-wall with projecting spear-points. Each clump of spearmen in the line would be neighbours who had come to war together, and they would be commanded by their local lord, their *thegn*, one of the knights of Anglo-Saxon England. Only at this rank – that of *thegn* – might men with swords be found.

Men treasured their swords, venerated them, even loved them. A good sword was the greatest gift that could be given in the mead-hall. 'Then Halfdane's son presented Beowulf with a gold standard as a victory gift, and embroidered banner; also breast-mail and a helmet; and a sword carried high, that was both precious object and token of honour.' It was the sword that ranked highest among the heroes of *Beowulf*.

The sword found by the river, of course, had a golden hilt. No mere *thegn* could have aspired to such a thing. Was it perhaps a gift from a king to an *ealdorman*?

Below: This sword from the Mound 1 ship-burial at Sutton Hoo shows what the North Lincolnshire sword may have looked like when complete.

A Warrior's Prized Possession

A spearhead could be fashioned in any village blacksmith's, but a sword was a pattern-welded steel blade. If it was less than this, it could shatter on impact and leave the man who wielded it weaponless in the chaos of mêlée. The centre of the blade was an iron strip, to which were welded two steel cutting-edges. On to either face were hammered layers of iron and steel twisted together, producing delicate decoration and an object of beauty. Swords were the finest achievement of the medieval armourer's art, and warriors treasured a good sword, for it could be the difference between life and death. 'Then he saw a blade that boded well,' recites the Anglo-Saxon poet in *Beowulf*, 'a sword in her armoury, an ancient heirloom from the days of the giants, an ideal weapon, one that any warrior would envy, but so huge and heavy of itself only Beowulf could wield it in battle.'

The World of the Mead-Hall

Anglo-Saxon kingship was sophisticated and simple at the same time. There was some of the bureaucracy and spin-doctoring of a modern state. Trade and diplomacy were elaborate and covered long distances. Craftsmanship and art were sometimes as good as anything the Romans had done. Yet Anglo-Saxon kings sat uneasily on wooden thrones at the end of a rowdy mead-hall. They were elected from among eligible candidates, but eligibility was often decided by the sword. They were tolerated by their barons only as long as they were graced with good fortune and success. Was the kingdom stable? Was it safe from attack? Were ranks and estates secure? Was the king rich enough to reward service well? One of our problems is that we tend to over-simplify the past, especially when sources are few; we try to impose an order on history that was never actually there. The kings and kingdoms that endured have left better records than the many that succumbed, so the former leave us with an impression of stability that was lacking at the time. Kings were frequently at war. Kingdoms rose and fell. Some great kings and many weak ones were slain on the battlefield, driven into exile or made the sub-kings of others. Each ruler therefore struggled to 'maintain confidence' at home: to convince his barons that he could lead them to victory.

Our key source for these mead-hall politics is the great Old English poem *Beowulf*. Though not written down before the early eighth century (and perhaps much later), it is an oral epic that developed over a long period. It is set in Denmark and combines Germanic myth with early sixth-century history, so the poem probably predates the Danish migrations and came to Britain in the memory of an Anglo-Saxon bard. It must then have evolved further, gaining among other things a Christian gloss, before finally taking its present written form. A characteristic of oral epic in traditional societies is that, while describing a lost heroic age of great warriors and mythic beasts, the setting of events tends to be one that is familiar to the audience. Beowulf himself, Grendel the man-eating monster, Grendel's vengeful mother, the fire-breathing dragon guarding its treasure: these are fiction. But mead-halls, fine weaponry, the code of honour, the value placed on martial prowess: these belong to the real world of the seventh century. From *Beowulf*, we learn several things about the politics of Anglo-Saxon kingship. The number and loyalty of the noble warriors in the king's retinue were crucial to royal power. The king attracted support through his reputation for success and generosity. There was an indissoluble link between victory, reward and honour. Victory meant booty, land, slaves, tribute – the wealth to pay for handsome gifts. Gifts of precious things – gold, swords, shirts of mail – were the rewards of loyal service and the measure of a man's honour. The king would live surrounded by this retinue: his *ealdormen* and *thegns* would feast with him, sleep in his hall, fight for him, and – or so it was hoped – die beside him if he should fall in battle. 'The fortunes of war favoured Hrothgar,' sings the poet in *Beowulf*. 'Friends and kinsmen flocked to his ranks, young followers, a force that grew to a mighty army.' So he built 'a great mead-hall', which was also 'a gift-hall', and here we find him in the midst of his retinue, a fountain of generosity to those who follow him, dispensing rings, torcs, helmets, shields, horse-harness, and much else. This is the lost world of Raedwald and the Sutton Hoo treasure, the world of the gem-encrusted sword from a Lincolnshire river, and of the mead-hall that once stood on Dave Cummings's field.

6 Cheap Trinkets of the Viking Settlers

Previous page and below: The ruins of the thirteenth-century Lindisfarne Priory on Holy Island. Nothing remains of the original monastery founded by St Aidan in 635, which was sacked by the Vikings.

Cheap Trinkets of the Viking Settlers

They struck first in the far north in AD 793. A small raiding party landed on Lindisfarne island to pillage and destroy the isolated monastery there. Further raids followed until, in 865, there was a full-scale invasion of East Anglia by what the chroniclers called 'the Great Army'. This time they stayed. Although their onslaught on Anglo-Saxon England was finally halted by King Alfred of Wessex at the battle of Edington in 878, the peace left King Guthrum and the Vikings in control of all the territory north and east of a line from Chester to London. This was the Danelaw. The *Anglo-Saxon Chronicle* records that in 879 'the host went from Cirencester into East Anglia, and occupied that land, and shared it out'. But what exactly does this mean? Were East Anglia and other parts of the Danelaw settled by large numbers of Danish farmers, or was there simply a parcelling out of estates among a new Danish aristocracy? This question has vexed students of the period for decades.

Ten years ago, the leading landscape archaeologist Tom Williamson, writing in his *Origins of Norfolk*, reflected the general view among East Anglia specialists:

> The *Chronicle's* statement that the Danes 'shared out' the county in 879 need imply no more than its division among a small conquering élite. The 'host' whose movements are described in tones of fascinated horror by the *Chronicle* was probably a fairly small band of fighting men, many of whom presumably returned to Denmark when the conquest was completed. There is no documentary evidence to suggest large-scale peasant immigration, and in Norfolk, as elsewhere in England, archaeological evidence for such a folk-movement is meagre.

Such Viking artefacts as had been found, Tom Williamson felt able to write off: '... these need indicate nothing more than trade with Scandinavia, or the presence of a Danish élite and the consequent prevalence of Danish taste.' This was the general view not just about East Anglia but the country as a whole. A few years earlier, the Southampton-based medieval specialist David Hinton, whose *Archaeology, Economy and Society* was a survey of settlement across England from the fifth to the fifteenth century, had written: '... there are [no] signs of a Danish culture in the rural Danelaw; stray finds of metalwork are infrequent and as likely to be found in English as in Danelaw England.'

All that, however, was before the metal-detector evidence had been published. The specialists were reflecting the fashion in historical explanation at the time. Invasions, conquests and colonization were out; instead the emphasis was on peaceful interaction and evolutionary change. But while it was true that none of the evidence *proved* large-scale Danish settlement – as opposed to 'élite domination' – some of it was suggestive. Apart from the historical records, there were impressive concentrations of Danish place names in parts of East Anglia and across much of Lincolnshire.

Scandinavian Remnants in Britain's Place Names

The name Grimston indicates an English village (-*ton*) taken over by a Scandinavian called 'Grimm'. The ending -by was the Scandinavian word for 'settlement'. There is a particular cluster of these on the Island of Flegg around Great Yarmouth, and Flegg itself was the Scandinavian word for 'reeds'. Or there are thorpe names, indicating secondary settlements, or those with kirk, meaning 'church', or beck, meaning 'stream'. Yet more significant are field names. Villages may be named by local nobles, but fields are unlikely to attract their attention, so field names are especially likely to reveal the language of the farmers who worked them. A study of the Flitcham area in north-west Norfolk has shown that many of the field names here are indeed Scandinavian – even though none of the major place names are. Many old Lincolnshire dialect words for landscape features are also Scandinavian – beck for 'stream', holme for 'island', carr for 'land' and gate for 'town street'.

Often, the regions with many Scandinavian words in names and speech are also those with large numbers of 'sokemen' recorded in the Domesday Book of 1086. In parts of Lincolnshire they formed over half the population, compared with less than 10 per cent in Essex. Sokemen were poor peasants but, unlike 'villeins', they were free men able to dispose of their own property. Could these be the descendants of free peasant settlers, demobilized from 'the Great Army', or arriving fresh from the Viking homeland in the wake of its conquests?

The problem had been the lack of finds from rural areas. Excavations at York, Lincoln, Norwich and elsewhere had revealed impressive evidence for Danish urbanism, but finds from the countryside had been restricted to a few items belonging to the military élite, such as swords and stirrup-mounts. By the mid 1990s, however, Kevin Leahy was reporting that 'our knowledge of Danish Lincolnshire has been revolutionized by the advent of the metal-detector, resulting in what has been, effectively, intensive fieldwalking of the whole of the county. Over 260 Viking and Anglo-Scandinavian objects have now been recorded.' It was the same story in Norfolk, where local archaeologists were reporting,

> the picture of the Viking presence … has been transformed by excavations, by fieldwork, and by metal-detecting. Numerous Viking objects found by members of the public have been brought to museums and archaeological units for identification and systematic recording, especially in Ipswich, Norwich, Lincoln and Scunthorpe. In the last ten years, the numbers of Viking-period finds have increased ten-fold, with about 200 recorded for Norfolk alone.

The specialists who saw these finds were struck by two things about them. First, the great majority were damaged or corroded: they were 'unstratified' plough-soil finds that had been torn from their original context and placed in a highly destructive environment. Recovering and recording these items was salvage archaeology. Second, the bulk of the material comprised cheap trinkets, mainly personal dress-fittings, and mainly for women. The technical terms for the Scandinavian styles of decoration used on the objects – 'Borre' and 'Jellinge' for Early Viking, 'Ringerike' and 'Urnes' for Late Viking – make them sound grand. The designs – somewhat angular knots, compressed interlace, and stark beast-heads – have real aesthetic appeal. However, the various brooches – trefoil, quadrangular, convex

Above: Enlarged details of a tenth-century trefoil brooch of copper alloy, decorated in 'Borre' style.

disc, flat disc, and so on – were crude artefacts of bronze. The poor quality of the metalwork implied that they were owned by peasants, not nobles, and the predominance of women's accessories strengthened the impression of wholesale folk-movement. Many of the objects were very similar to examples found in Denmark. The distribution pattern was also similar in the two countries. These Viking brooches were not found in hoards or local concentrations, but one by one over a wide area – as if they were the low-value possessions (thus not hoarded) of a peasant population (so, widely scattered) that were sometimes accidentally lost (hence turning up as individual finds).

All archaeologists know that distribution maps are dodgy things. A map of Britain with groups of dots here and there and blank spaces in between is presented as if it depicted the past – the distribution of Iron Age torcs, Romano-Celtic temples or Late Anglo-Saxon stirrup-strap mounts Class A Type 10B. Even worse, one distribution map gets compared with another, to prove that chalk and cheese are the same. What the maps actually show, of course, is where people have found certain things. Before we can turn this into an image of the past, we have to negotiate the elephant traps on the road to archaeological interpretation. We have to remember that while some things survive in the soil to become evidence on a distribution map – such as stone buildings – other things may not – such as timber ones; and also that while a certain thing may survive well in some conditions, it may disappear completely in others – notably wood or bone. Then there are the numbers of finders, who may be many in some places, and few elsewhere, so that our distribution turns out to be a distribution of amateur fieldwalkers or university archaeology departments. Meanwhile, finders also know that some areas are easy to explore – the thin, loose, well-drained soils of chalk downland – and other places harder – wet, clay-filled valleys where the archaeology is deep and hard to dig.

Kevin Leahy knows the problem. 'The first question,' he says about interpreting results, 'is whether or not the distribution of the metal-detector finds is coherent or if, as has been the case in the past, it reflects only concentrations of fieldwork.' So he tested the distribution of Dark Age metalwork recovered by detectorists in Lincolnshire against the evidence of the Domesday Book. There was a close match. The areas largely without metal finds were recorded by Domesday as sparsely settled woodland, coastal marsh or fen. Metal-detectorists were finding Viking artefacts where William the Conqueror's commissioners recorded settlement. There were so many metal-detectorists, and so many finds being recorded, that the archaeological sample recovered was, it turned out, a genuinely representative one for Lincolnshire as a whole. It can be taken as highly significant, then, that the distribution of Viking metalwork recorded in Lincolnshire ties in well with the incidence of Scandinavian place names and Domesday sokemen. The evidence here – and in Norfolk – for large-scale settlement by Danish peasant-farmers in the late ninth and tenth centuries is now very compelling. The Vikings are finally emerging from the darkness of Britain's past.

And in this there are lessons to be learnt about the use of metal-detectors in archaeology and what we mean by 'treasure'.

What is treasure?

There is an evolving legal definition of treasure in England and Wales. It used to mean bullion and an assertion of the king's right to any that was found. Later it came to mean ancient objects of gold and silver that were admired by antiquarians and art lovers. And

most recently, as defined in the Treasure Act of 1996, the definition has been expanded to cover many other metallic objects, either found in association with gold and silver, or of such antiquity that they are deemed especially valuable in their own right. The new meaning of 'treasure' bears the hallmarks of its legal antecedents. It is a compromise between medieval greed for gold, nineteenth-century connoisseurship and modern heritage professionalism.

There is also a popular definition – or perhaps two. Hoards of bullion buried but never recovered are the stuff of numerous adventure stories like Robert Louis Stevenson's *Treasure Island* or the Humphrey Bogart film *The Treasure of the Sierra Madre*. The quest is an exciting challenge, the rewards at its end a source of conflict, and everyone is fascinated by the sudden acquisition of fabulous wealth. There is something of this – but also something more – in the popular appeal of great archaeological discoveries. When Schliemann excavated the shaft-graves of Mycenae in 1876, or Carter the tomb of Tutankhamun in 1922, the world was aghast – not just because of the huge hauls of precious and beautiful objects, but because of their antiquity and the past worlds for which they

Left: Long John Silver (Robert Newton) examines his finds in the 1950 film version of Treasure Island.

stood testimony. What was truly awesome was that the objects were found in the burial chambers of Mycenaean warlords and an Egyptian pharaoh from the second millennium BC. And herein lies their real value: the information they contain about a lost world.

The gold bullion stashed in modern banks arouses little general interest. The ingots are anonymous lumps of metal. They tell no story. They open no portals into history. The real excitement about treasures from antiquity is that they are the silent witnesses to human action in a distant past. Because of that, the market value of a bullion hoard is less important to most of us – who are never destined to find one – than the knowledge contained in a scatter of cheap trinkets. None of the finders featured in this book ever expected to strike gold. The vast majority of detectorists never have such luck, and certainly never become rich. Most do not cover the cost of their batteries, let alone their detectors. What drives them is an interest in the past. In addition, while spectacular discoveries like Cliff Bradshaw's golden goblet or Alan Meek's silver figurine tell us a lot, the systematic recording of much larger numbers of everyday objects can tell us much more. Thanks to Cliff, we know that a great Bronze Age lord was buried beneath a barrow in eastern Kent. Thanks to Alan, we have learnt the name of a new Celtic goddess and found her watery shrine on the edge of the Chilterns. And thanks to dozens of others recovering and reporting battered bits from the plough-lands of eastern England, we now know that a thousand years ago it was full of Danes. This knowledge is the real 'hidden treasure' – and anyone can join in the search.

7 Joining the Search for Hidden Treasure

Previous page: The poorly excavated and heavily ploughed site of Poor Lot barrows, a Bronze Age cemetery near Winterbourne Abbas in Dorset.
Below: Modern excavation in progress at Wallsend, Newcastle-upon-Tyne.

Joining the Search for Hidden Treasure

A short while ago, TV archaeologist Julian Richards argued in *BBC History Magazine* that metal-detecting is 'the wholesale hoovering up of artefacts from the field into private collections or on to the commercial market', and that this is 'both morally wrong and, when carried out by untrained hands, cannot fail to cause great damage to our archaeological heritage'. Likening the hobby to collecting birds' eggs or digging up wild orchids, he continued:

> I have two main arguments against metal-detecting. The first is that, in the majority of cases, information about the context of an object is irretrievably lost. … The second concerns responsibilities. I have to make sure before I dig up any artefact that I have the resources to ensure that it is conserved, studied, published and eventually stored in an appropriate place where it is available to all to view or examine. But a metal-detectorist can dig up an object in the expectation that the resources of the archaeological and museum world will swing into action.

This view is widespread among archaeologists. It will be clear that I do not share it. Taking birds' eggs or wild orchids destroys a living part of the environment. Taking artefacts from the plough-soil rescues them from eventual destruction. To metal-detect may, therefore, be academically desirable and morally commendable. There is a sharp distinction to be drawn between what has sometimes been called 'conscientious detecting' and various more disreputable practices ranging from vandalism due to ignorance to wholesale criminal looting. There is also, let it be said, a distinction to be made between good and bad archaeological practice. Some of the people throwing stones live in glass houses. For ten years now we have had a 'free market' in development-driven archaeology, with rescue units forced to compete with one another for contracts. The results are entirely as predicted. Units win tenders by cutting costs. Professional archaeologists face job insecurity, low pay, poor conditions and dismal prospects. There is pressure on site directors and supervisors to get work done cheaply and fast. Machines are used more than they should be. Only 'samples' of sites are actually dug. Corners are cut in post-excavation, and photostatted 'grey literature' replaces proper publication accessible to all. Strong, geographically based units – with extensive archives, detailed local knowledge and specialists rooted in the area – lose sites on their own patch to cowboy contractors doing smash-and-grab work. Much modern rescue work is, of course, much better than this, but where the anarchy of the market rules some is certainly very bad.

And these are the sites that *are* investigated. Alongside them are huge numbers of others being lost to processes not covered by planning controls. Many are being destroyed by tidal erosion on our coasts. Others by water-extraction and the desiccation of wetlands. Yet more by quarrying. But the biggest danger by far is modern cultivation. In the last 50 years, thousands of earthwork features in the British landscape have been ploughed flat, and each year further ploughing, often deeper than ever, cuts away the upper layers of thousands of buried archaeological sites. The coins, brooches and potsherds incorporated in plough-soil are testimony to that destruction. These objects are some kind of record of what has been lost and what may still lie undisturbed. Once in the plough-soil, of course, these objects, having perhaps been more or less stable for centuries, become vulnerable to rapid disintegration. Air, water, fertilizers, pesticides and repeated battering by machines will eventually destroy them.

Developers pay for professional work on rescue sites covered by the planning process. There is no one to pay professionals to work on most other threatened sites. Nor is there anyone to pay for much research elsewhere. The old idea that you should not dig unthreatened sites because there were so many threatened ones demanding attention is now rejected. No academic research programme should be driven by the construction industry. If we only collect data where new roads are being built, we end up collecting the data for its own sake without any wider purpose. As soon as we start thinking about the past and hypothesizing about how it worked, we have to seek out the most appropriate sites to test our theories.

A good example is the new Whittlewood project. Chris Dyer, a Leicester-based professor who describes himself as 'a social and economic historian with archaeological interests', studies medieval settlements. The problem he faced was that most of his evidence came from the failures: so-called 'deserted medieval villages' (or DMVs) that were now greenfield sites and therefore open to archaeological investigation. What about villages that did not disappear, the successful ones where there is a still a village today? These were avoided because they were so much harder to explore – but they might well have a very different story to tell. So several years ago Chris launched the Whittlewood project, which is investigating medieval settlement in a dozen parishes straddling the Buckinghamshire/Northamptonshire border. The idea is to find out when different parts of existing villages came into use by going into people's gardens and digging 1-square-metre (10-square-foot) test pits. Features are recorded and collections of potsherds analysed to work out when things were happening. Archaeologist Richard Jones has already supervised 150 test pits – dug mainly by local volunteers and students – while historian colleague Mark Page concentrates on putting the archaeology into context by studying the documents and maps for the area. The DMVs and other earthwork sites are also being recorded to build up a comprehensive picture of medieval settlement over the whole area. It is pure research, it depends heavily on volunteers, and it is probably the most important thing happening in medieval settlement studies at the present time.

The amount of archaeological material is vast. There are numerous sites in every parish, many of which are deteriorating. Others that are safe for the time being contain the answers to important questions. Only a fraction of the work that needs to be done can be covered by professionals. There is work for an army of volunteers to help recover the heritage locked up in the British landscape. Professional archaeologists should be the organizers and facilitators of that army – this is part of the moral obligation they carry as the custodians of a heritage that belongs to all.

There are moral obligations, too, on those who become amateur detectorists, field-walkers or excavators. Obligations, however, are not necessarily burdens. On the contrary, for those whose hobby is investigating the past, to work in a 'conscientious' way is to enhance its rewards. If artefacts are safely recovered and properly conserved, if undisturbed archaeological deposits are investigated only by controlled excavation, if find-spots are properly recorded and artefacts assigned a proper context – if these things happen, for most amateurs the thrill of their hobby increases. Many detectorists, for instance, find their way into other forms of archaeology: fieldwalking, joining excavations, attending courses at local colleges, becoming experts in certain classes of object.

So how do you join the search, and what are the obligations of 'conscientious' recovery if you do?

Learning As You Go

Trevor Austin is a retired heating engineer who lives with his wife in a village a few miles outside Doncaster. He hated history at school, but became fascinated by it later in life and for over 20 years has been an active detectorist. 'I was staggered there was so much in the ground to be found. To actually find, let us say, a coin that belonged to a Roman soldier. That's fantastic. That's the attraction for many people. Who dropped it? What were they doing?' Trevor is now the general secretary of the National Council for Metal Detecting (NCMD), and was heavily involved in negotiations over the new Treasure Act and the launch of the Portable Antiquities Scheme. He was also a key adviser to the BBC in developing the *Hidden Treasure* series. He and the NCMD are firm supporters of conscientious detecting and co-operation with archaeologists, and equally firm opponents of nighthawking and the destruction of heritage sites. What advice does he give to those who want to join the hobby?

Don't just go out and buy the first detector you come across. Join a club, talk to people there, get to know what type of metal-detector people are using, what the pros and cons of different machines are. Don't go out and buy the most expensive machine. It will probably be too sophisticated and you may find it difficult to get to grips with. Certainly to start with, a 'switch on and go' machine will do fine. Two or three hundred pounds would buy you a good, basic, second-hand machine of this type, maybe twice that for a new one.

Metal-detecting is one way of joining the search for hidden treasure. Another is to join a field research project or an amateur archaeology society. Many of

Left: Trevor Austin, general secretary of the National Council for Metal Detecting, at a detectorists' rally.

these groups welcome new members keen to undertake fieldwork, and any that do not, perhaps because they have become inactive, may simply need a push. Research projects are often run as training digs, and even some that are not may encourage new volunteers and offer informal 'learning as you go'. The best source of information is *The Archaeology Handbook*, an annual directory issued by the popular magazine *Current Archaeology* (see 'Suggested Reading'). There is often something for everybody – one of the attractive features of archaeology is that it employs a wide range of different techniques. These break down into three areas of activity that often follow one another sequentially. First comes 'desktop' research. This means using documents, maps, aerial photos and records of earlier discoveries either to find out about a site where fieldwork is planned or to gain new insights by synthesizing data already available.

The second area is new fieldwork. This might be 'non-invasive' and involve surface activities like fieldwalking, metal-detecting, mapping earthworks, geophysical surveys, analysing old buildings for structural phases, and investigating boundaries through field reconnaissance and counting the species in hedgerows. 'Invasive' fieldwork, on the other hand, means a process of excavation that destroys the evidence as it exposes and records it. All excavation involves 'sampling' – we are always digging parts of some greater whole – but the samples may be small and scattered ('test pits'), larger and more targeted ('trial trenches') or selected fractions of a site which are fully exposed ('open area').

The third area is 'post-excavation'. Finds – potsherds, animal bones, metalwork, snail shells, carbonized seeds – have to be identified, analysed as an assemblage, and then interpreted for the light they throw on the site. The records of fieldwork – written notes, drawings, measurements, photographs – also have to be written up, integrated with finds data, and then turned into a full, finished report.

There is a tendency in archaeology – as in all professions – to create a certain mystique around the techniques employed in order to enhance the status of qualified practitioners. Do not be hoodwinked. Site directors, who oversee the whole process, are often highly skilled, as are many of their supervisors, but formal qualifications count for far less than experience. This is because archaeology is always based on material – landscapes, earthworks, old walls, layers of soil, bone fragments, broken crockery, bits of brooches. Archaeology has its theoretical side, but be suspicious of anything called 'archaeological theory' that is not firmly rooted in material evidence. You can learn

Above: Sally Worrell, finds advisor for Prehistoric and Roman Artefacts with the Institute of Archaeology, helping interested amateurs on a typical Open Day.

about the *results* of archaeology in a lecture theatre, but you can only learn how *to do* archaeology in the field. It is long experience of digging sites or handling artefacts that makes for a good archaeologist. The basics, on the other hand – what you need to know to get started – are easy. This is true even of excavation, where most people become competent trowellers and make themselves useful on site after a few days; and those keen to learn will often find, at least on the better volunteer digs, that they are encouraged to carry out detailed recording with minimal supervision after a week or two. There is, in short, a role for everyone.

Here are some basic rules for the conscientious amateur. They are written mainly with metal-detectorists in mind, since other amateurs are likely to work as part of a larger team under some sort of archaeological direction. The ethical principles, however, apply to all.

1. Work only with permission

All land is owned. You need to find out who the owner is and get permission before carrying out any work. This is even true of common land – such as footpaths, parks, and the foreshore – which, as public property, is administered by government bodies. Be aware that much land is subject to further constraints. Regardless of ownership, for instance, Scheduled Ancient Monuments are protected heritage sites, and Sites of Special Scientific Interest are protected natural environments. To search these sites you need permission from official government bodies. Once you have the necessary permissions, you must be aware of and respect the rules, formal and informal, governing the land where you are working. In the countryside, you should not leave gates open, damage crops, frighten animals, cause a fire hazard, drop litter or leave open holes. It is also advisable to make an agreement beforehand about the ownership of finds. Common practice is that any rewards for treasure should be equally divided between finder and landowner. Be aware that your local museum may well be interested in acquiring some of your finds. Try to build up a relationship with a curator and keep him or her informed about your activities.

2. Metal-detect only disturbed topsoil deposits

There are millions of ancient metallic artefacts in British plough-soil. About 90 per cent of metal-detected finds are from cultivated land, and virtually all of these come from the plough-churned topsoil. Finds from this level are what archaeologists call 'unstratified' because they have been removed from their original 'context'. It is desirable to recover such finds *provided they are properly recorded*. Some other topsoil deposits have also been formed or turned over in recent times. Coastal sand and mud deposits are obvious examples. Where recent deposition or disturbance is certain, it is acceptable to recover finds here also. What you should not remove are finds from 'stratified' deposits, where objects are still embedded in archaeological layers. Occasionally, if ground has not been disturbed for a very long time, or if erosion has removed much of the topsoil, stratified finds may lie close to the surface. Alternatively, your detector may pick up a signal from an object that turns out to be deeply buried. If it is beneath the plough-soil, you will – if you look carefully – often notice a distinct soil change and realize that the artefact lies in a deposit somewhat different in colour, composition and compaction to the overlying plough-soil. An even clearer indication of an *in situ* deposit would be to find several artefacts together, forming a hoard. Why is this important? Because a stratified artefact has a position within a sequence of archaeological layers that means it is still part of a story. It can tell us much more as part of that story than it ever could on its own. So there are two basic rules: avoid seeking artefacts sealed within stratified deposits; and if you accidentally strike one too important to be ignored, consult your local finds liaison officer (FLO) who can bring in specialist help for a controlled excavation if appropriate. Be sensible: it is pretty obvious when you are getting out of your depth.

3. Recover finds with care

Ideally, finds should not be dug out from immediately above, and they should certainly not be levered or yanked free of the ground. The best policy is to work the soil from *around* them until their extent is clearly defined, when they can be removed by gently undercutting the soil beneath them. Each find should be separately bagged and labelled. The bags should be the sealable type (available in all good detector shops), punctured with ventilation holes, provided with extra padding if necessary, and labelled using a permanent marker. All finds should be kept in a polythene box, and this should be padded to prevent them rattling around and suffering damage. Finds should not be cleaned in the field except for the gentle removal of obvious surface soil.

4. Record and report all finds

Metal-detectorists, fieldwalkers, excavators and others working in the field have an obligation to record discoveries accurately and report them fully to local archaeological authorities, usually the FLO. This, anyway, has the great benefit of assistance with identification and access to additional information to put discoveries into context. This is also the best way to deal with suspected treasure. Finds liaison officers are now established in all parts of England and Wales, and they are fully competent to advise on treasure and basic conservation and storage, as well as to record routine finds.

Detectorists are strongly urged to take grid-references of find-spots to at least six figures (though eight is better). A six-figure reference is accurate to within 100 square metres (approximately 1,000 square feet), an eight-figure one to within 10 square metres (100 square feet). The easiest way to take a grid-reference is to use a hand-held Global Positioning System (GPS) device, which works off satellites; these are now relatively cheap and give very accurate results. Surveys show that even on sites ploughed for centuries most objects do not move very far, so precise plotting of find-spots can be very rewarding as it gradually reveals the hidden form of a site. The grid-reference should be clearly marked on the finds bag. Finds with a 'provenance' (an accurate find-spot) are much more archaeologically valuable than those without.

Many detectorists are justifiably concerned that archaeologists keep some find-spots confidential – a sensible precaution against nighthawks. However, archaeologists share their concern fully and have long experience of restricting detailed information about find-spots to *bona fide* researchers with a need to know. Finders should therefore provide full information and indicate when they feel it is sensitive. Finds can either be taken periodically to the local museum for identification and recording, or this can be done through a local detecting club with which the FLO is in contact. Common practice is for finds to be retained by the FLO for a set period until a full record has been made, at which point they are returned to the finder. FLOs have no legal right to hold finds that have been voluntarily handed over, so there is no risk of finds not being returned.

5. Conserve and curate finds properly

Archaeological finds are often fragile and liable to decay. Conservation is a highly skilled job dependent on detailed knowledge of chemistry and access to expensive equipment. Many 'common-sense' procedures for cleaning and conserving finds may in fact be very destructive. Finders are strongly recommended not to rely on amateur tips passed on at clubs or in hobby magazines, but to read some of the more accessible literature produced by professional conservators. With the right advice, there is much you can do cheaply and successfully at home; but many procedures – including some once used by professionals which research has now shown to be flawed – can cause irreparable damage or corrosion. To treat finds badly is to reduce their historical, aesthetic and financial value. Washing finds under the tap, drying them in the airing cupboard, scrubbing them with brushes to clean them, dowsing them in Dettol or Coca-Cola to remove corrosion, coating them in wax or oil to keep out the damp: all these and many other common procedures can be destructive. If you want to join the search for the past, you must teach yourself how to look after finds. Museums and FLOs can advise, but there is also now an excellent book, *Guide to Conservation for Metal Detectorists* (see 'Suggested Reading'). You also have a responsibility to store and, if you choose to, display finds so that they remain stable and safe. This also requires some specialist knowledge. Some fixatives – like reusable adhesive putty – can be very damaging. Again, the same book offers much useful advice.

Constructive Co-operation

Imagine a ban on metal-detectors. Imagine a wider ban on all amateur fieldwork. Imagine a situation in which the state controlled all archaeology and issued licences to work on archaeological sites only to approved practitioners. What would be the effect?

Some things would not change at all. Sites would still be raided in the night and antiquities looted for sale on the black market. Other sites might be explored by determined hobbyists and landowners prepared to cock a snook at the law in return for a cut – but the finds, of course, would never be reported. The wholesale destruction of archaeology by natural processes, uncontrolled development and modern ploughing would continue. There would still be shoddy work by outside contractors undercutting local units, and an archaeological proletariat of badly paid young graduates moving from one insecure job to another.

Other things, however, would change dramatically. Tens of thousands of people would have their hobby and their pathway into history and heritage shut off. Dozens of sites that might have been explored would remain unknown, and tens of thousands of artefacts would be left to rot in plough-soil. The flow of new entries on county records would slow to a trickle. Planning archaeologists, monitoring redevelopment, would know less about the

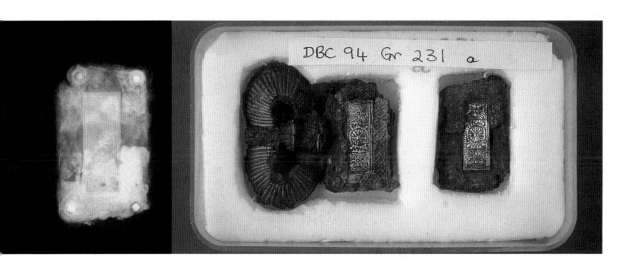

Above: A lesson in the dangers of mistreating finds. A corroded, misshapen lump of metal (left) is shown by X-ray (centre) to be an elaborately decorated Frankish buckle set made of composite materials. Only highly skilled conservation work could recover this object (right) from its casing of rust .

sites in the way of construction work, and research archaeologists would have an attenuated database.

It is time to erase the lines in the sand that have often divided professionals from amateurs, and archaeologists from detectorists. The real line is between the great majority who want to share constructively in the recovery of our heritage and are prepared to work co-operatively to achieve it, and a small minority who are in it for the money.

Appendix

The most pressing question for everyone who finds treasure is: what happens to the finds? Are they, for a start, technically 'treasure'? This is a legal term that dates back probably to Anglo-Saxon times, and the law of 'treasure trove' in force until 1997 was a ridiculous survival from the thirteenth century. The essence of the law was that objects of gold or silver that had been deliberately hidden with the intention of recovery qualified as 'treasure trove' and became the property of the Crown once discovered. Nice if you were the king – except that any finder with common sense would just keep quiet. By Victorian times, there was another problem: the bullion value of 'treasure' – even it *was* declared – was insignificant as a source of revenue to the state compared with the historical interest it aroused among the growing fraternity of gentleman antiquarians. So the law was modified, and from 1886 onwards finds deemed to be 'treasure trove' were offered to museums, and finders were paid a reward for them. But the law was still an ass. Right up until 1997 there would be learned debates at coroners' inquests to decide whether a pit full of Iron Age bullion was, in effect, an unclaimed safe-deposit box or a ritual offering to the gods. If the former, the museum got it; if the latter, the finder. It all depended on the supposed intentions of someone who had been dead for 2,000 years. This creaking medieval legal edifice was finally brought down by a piece of twentieth-century technology: the metal-detector.

Basic detectors became relatively cheap and easily obtainable in the 1970s, and a new hobby quickly took off. No one really knows how many people got involved, but for a while it may have been tens of thousands before the numbers settled down to the present total of up to 15,000 at the most. Many of these are dedicated detectorists who go out most weeks and are active members of local clubs. The hobby is now highly organized. There are about 150 clubs affiliated to the National Council for Metal Detecting

(NCMD), and a typical club will regularly draw 20 or 30 members to its monthly meetings. Many other detectorists, who are not members of clubs and work independently, belong to the Federation of Independent Detectorists (FID). Most are dedicated to history, many are very knowledgeable, some have followed archaeology courses or worked on digs. There are two good hobby magazines – *The Searcher* and *Treasure Hunting* – but many detectorists read far more widely. The National Council promotes best practice, 'conscientious detecting', good relations with archaeologists and the proper reporting of finds. But it was not always thus. When the hobby started the situation was sometimes chaotic. What happened at Wanborough near Guildford in Surrey was nothing short of a scandal.

What Objects Qualify as Treasure?

Coins
All coins from the same find (two or more) provided they are at least 300 years old when found. If they contain less than 10 per cent gold or silver, there must be at least ten of them.

Metal objects
All prehistoric base-metal objects from the same find (two or more).
All finds (one or more) at least 300 years old and containing 10 per cent or more gold or silver.

Associated finds
Any object, whatever it is made of, found in the same place as (or having previously been together with) another object that is treasure.

A trial trench in the 1970s had revealed a length of curving Roman masonry. Shortly afterwards, metal-detectorists found a number of Iron Age coins in the hedge-bank that bordered the nearby country lane. These were properly reported, but at the treasure trove inquest the exact location of the find-spot was revealed. This led to a frenzied treasure hunt in which an estimated 10,000 or 20,000 Iron Age coins were looted, dispersed and often sold abroad. None of them was recorded. From an archaeological point of view, these coins might as well never have existed. A piece of everyone's heritage had been stolen. Later excavations at Wanborough revealed it to have been a major Iron Age and Roman sanctuary – but now with a great chunk of the jigsaw missing.

Wanborough – and other sites which archaeologists regarded as 'under attack' – created a lot of bitterness about metal-detecting in general. There were calls for it to be banned – for the machines to be made illegal. The Surrey Archaeological Society – whose patch included Wanborough – was in the forefront of the campaign, and the Council for British Archaeology launched the so-called 'STOP' campaign ('Stop Taking Our Past'). There were scare stories in the archaeological press about the threat to sites, the number of 'portable antiquities' that were being taken out of the ground, and the flow of these into the hands of dealers and foreign collectors. It was claimed that several hundred thousand antiquities a year were being dug up, and only a tiny percentage were getting reported. One result was that pressure built up against the old law of treasure trove. As it stood, it offered no guaranteed protection to sites like Wanborough; indeed, in this case, none whatsoever – it was established that Wanborough was a sanctuary and, since ritual deposits were not intended to be recovered by the original owners, the coins would have been deemed to belong to their present-day finders.

Lord Perth introduced a Treasure Bill into Parliament in 1994 as a private member. This was hailed by *The Times* with the headline 'Peer aims to save heritage from metal-detectors'. It was an exaggeration, but it reflected the general bias: the Surrey Archaeological Society was one of Perth's key advisers. The NCMD, the FID, the two hobby magazines and other groups representing metal-detectorists (and dealers) came out against the proposed bill. Local MPs were lobbied by constituents who were detectorists, and the government backed away from an ugly row. But there was clearly still a problem. The status quo was untenable. However, a legal clampdown on detecting, let alone a complete ban, was not an attractive option. Was there another way?

The problem was complex, and archaeologists were not in agreement. There were several strands of opinion. The most forceful came from those who regarded metal-detectors as a menace and believed they should be banned; probably, at the time, this was the majority view among archaeologists. But another group feared that any ban would simply drive metal-detecting underground. There was a demand for looted antiquities and there were dealers prepared to pay good prices for them, which meant that, whatever the law, sites would continue to be attacked for commercial gain. The black market operates outside the law so any ban would affect the hobbyists, not the crooks. This was a critical distinction. Metal-detectors are tools. They can be used to loot antiquities for profit, and they can be used to save antiquities from the plough. Hopeless confusion has reigned in the minds of many archaeologists, especially of the older generation, through the failure to make this distinction. But a minority of young archaeologists understood it from the outset. They were criticized for this at the time, and they deserve credit for it now: as it turns out, they were the pioneers of an intelligent and highly productive relationship between detectorists and archaeologists, a relationship now enshrined in a new Treasure Act and, complementing it, the extraordinarily successful Portable Antiquities Scheme.

What Should I Do if I Find Something that May Be Treasure?

You must report all finds of treasure to the coroner for the district in which the finds were made, either within 14 days of the day on which you made the find, or within 14 days after the day on which you realized that the find might be treasure (for example, as a result of having it identified). The obligation to report finds applies to everyone, including archaeologists.

'They do different', we are told, in Norfolk. Sometimes this may be a good thing. Perhaps the most prominent of the young archaeologists who championed metal-detecting was the Norfolk archaeologist Tony Gregory. Tony was a bit of a rebel. *Current Archaeology* described him as 'one of the leading archaeologists of the perhaps somewhat anarchic generation that graduated in the 1960s and 70s. With hair everywhere, his shirt stripped open down to the navel, he concealed a very sharp intellect under an unconventional exterior.' Born in Nottingham, educated at the local grammar school, he went to Cambridge in 1968 to study archaeology and anthropology. This could have been a disaster. In those days, students 'reading' archaeology at Cambridge were not encouraged to undertake fieldwork. Presumably it was not considered necessary for young gentlemen. Fortunately, Tony had been digging since 1966 at the Iron Age and Roman settlement site at Dragonby in Lincolnshire. After graduation, he went straight to work as an archaeologist, and in 1974 he began his career in Norfolk when he got a job at the Norwich Castle

Left: A typical photo of Tony Gregory, among the first archaeologists to champion the hobby of metal-detecting.

Museum. The county was big and archaeologically rich, and a growing proportion of the finds coming into the museum at the time had been metal-detected. Tony's job included identifying finds brought in by members of the public and logging the significant ones for inclusion in the Sites and Monuments Record (SMR), thereby helping to build up a full catalogue of all the archaeological discoveries in the country. He therefore had to work out his own response to the new hobby. It was distinctive, as his friend and colleague Andrew Rogerson explains:

He soon realized that metal objects brought in for identification and recording were frequently the result of deliberate searching with detectors, and that if the obvious enthusiasms of a growing number of detector-users were to be harnessed in the right direction, then the archaeological databank for the county would be vastly enhanced. Thus he began to foster close liaisons with detectorists, to encourage correct procedures of recording and to inform finders through his uniquely entertaining yet brilliantly intellectual methods of identification. All of this he did for two reasons: a strong desire to see information recorded in order to further knowledge, and a genuine affection for the rich variety of characters who pursue the detecting hobby. He was thus an academic of the highest calibre as well as a popularizer with the 'common touch'.

How Do I Report a Find of Treasure?

Very simply. You may report your find to the coroner in person, by letter, telephone, fax, or e-mail. The coroner or his officer will send you an acknowledgement and tell you where you should deposit your find.

In each coroner's district there is a local agreement between the coroner, the finds liaison officer, local government archaeological officers and local or national museums, about where treasure finds should be deposited. From December 2003, a national network of FLOs will have been established across the whole of England and Wales. The FLOs will then be the main point of contact for treasure finds.

The finds liaison officer or the museum or local government archaeological officer receiving the find will give you a receipt. They will need to know exactly where you made the find. You and the landowner should keep the find-site location confidential. The body or individual receiving the find will notify the Sites and Monuments Record as soon as possible (if that has not already happened), so that the site where the find was made can be investigated by archaeologists if necessary.

Tony Gregory quickly emerged as a leading champion and friend of the hobby. He and Norfolk colleagues faced impassioned criticism, but they stood their ground. 'The metal-detector is an electronic instrument; it is incapable of any independent act of will,' wrote Gregory and Rogerson in an acerbic article in the journal *Antiquity*. 'It is outside the reference of a system of good or evil: it is neither benign nor malign, ethical or unethical, as neutral in such matters as a stone. It is capable merely of indicating the presence of certain objects on or below the soil. It bears no responsibility for human action consequent upon such indications.' The implication was that responsible metal-detecting was a positive boon, and the article went on to describe recent Norfolk examples. Two things were happening in the county. First, detectorists were not only being encouraged to report their finds; they were being positively welcomed as people contributing knowledge. Second, they were being invited to take part in projects run by county archaeologists. In Tony Gregory's view, for instance, 'All previously excavated examples of material from Late Iron Age and Early Roman sites should be considered as having grossly under-represented assemblages of metalwork because detectors were not used.' In other words, if you do not detect on your excavations, you will miss most of the metalwork. The reason is simple enough: most of it is in bulk deposits which get removed by machines or heavy tools; and even metalwork in carefully excavated deposits often gets missed by trowellers.

The figures speak for themselves. By the late 1990s, Norfolk archaeologists had regular contact with four of the five detecting clubs in the county. The mutual trust was such that museum staff would attend monthly meetings, collect the new finds, take them away for recording, and return them at the following meeting. They were getting to see around 25,000 finds a year, of which about half were significant and were being entered on the county database. This meant there were probably as many metal-detected finds being recorded in Norfolk as in the rest of the country put together. A few other places – Suffolk, Hertfordshire, Kent, Leicestershire, North Lincolnshire – had by now developed similar schemes and were catching up, but most of the country was still a desert. Tens of thousands of archaeological artefacts were being saved from the plough – but without record.

Back in London, caught up in the rumpus caused by the Treasure Bill, was an urbane museum curator called Roger Bland. Suited and respectable, he was at home in the committee rooms of the British Museum and the new Department of National Heritage. He also had a lot of common sense. He had not gone along with the howling antipathy to metal-detectorists that had been heard from some of the archaeological profession. Museum people often have a better grip on reality than unit archaeologists. They have more contact with the public because they are at the display end of things. Museums are parts of communities: people come into them to see what has been found, kids to do their work sheet on the Romans and finders to get an ID on objects dug up in their garden – or metal-detected in a farmer's field. Roger could see both sides. He was a moderate in a highly polarized situation. Sites were being vandalized and finds were unreported, but a lot of useful data was being collected and many people's lives were being enriched by the hobby. There was also an unsavoury air of élitism about the anti lobby. Quite a few professional archaeologists at the time were pushing for the exclusion of all amateurs – whether metal-detectorists or volunteer excavators. There was a danger of heritage being turned into the preserve of a self-appointed clique of 'experts'.

It was Roger who brought in the NCMD. Its leaders were invited to join government-level discussions, and in 1995 they produced a considered written response to Lord Perth's proposed Treasure Bill. 'As a result,' Roger explains, 'the bill's sponsors made five amendments to meet their concerns, and ministers stated during debates in Parliament that the government had no intention of banning or otherwise restricting responsible metal-detecting, and nor was it the first step down a road which would eventually result in the compulsory reporting of all finds or the licensing of all detector users.' The new Treasure Act came into force in September 1997.

What Happens if my Find Is Treasure?

If the finds liaison officer, museum curator or archaeologist believes that the find may be treasure, they will inform the British Museum or the National Museum of Wales. They will then decide whether they or any other museum wishes to acquire it from the Crown.

If a museum wants to acquire a find, the coroner will hold an inquest to decide whether the find is treasure. You, the site occupier and the landowner will be invited to attend and will able to question witnesses at the inquest.

If the find is declared to be treasure, it will be taken to the British Museum or the National Museum of Wales to be valued by the Treasure Valuation Committee.

Around 25 finds a year were being declared Treasure Trove under the old law; that total leapt to 205 in the first year of the new one (1997–8), and now stands at 302 (2001–02). The great majority of new finds, however, would have counted as treasure under the old law, so it looks as if far more people are now declaring their finds.

The Treasure Act was only part, and quite a small part, of the reformed approach to portable antiquities. It was not intended to deal with the tens of thousands of routine finds made every year mainly, but not exclusively, by metal-detectorists – objects museums did not want. Even under the Treasure Act, nearly half the items declared were returned to the finders without an inquest because no museum wished to acquire them. Most metal-detected finds were small, battered, corroded and unexceptional. Thousands of Roman coins, most of them worth only a few pounds on the market, came up each year. They were certainly not display items. There were usually other examples in reserve collections, and museums generally were short of storage space. It was not the individual objects that mattered, but the overall quantities and the distribution patterns – and the knowledge that could be obtained from recording these objects *en masse*. A law to nationalize all antiquities – saying they all belonged to the state – would have been pointless. It would have been unenforceable, and anyway the state did not want them. A law banning metal-detectors – saying people were not allowed to collect the antiquities – would have been absurd for a different reason. Undetected material would eventually disintegrate to nothing in plough-soil. What was the good of that to anyone? There was really only one outstanding issue. If the Norfolk system was to go national, should reporting be compulsory or voluntary?

The government issued a discussion document and invited comments. Only a small percentage of objects found by the public were being recorded by museums, it explained, and 'this represents a considerable loss to the nation's heritage. Once an object has left the ground and lost its provenance, a large part of its archaeological value is lost. The result is a loss of information about the past which is irreplaceable.' There were 174 responses, roughly equally divided between archaeologists and metal-detectorists, and a consensus in favour of a voluntary scheme. The arguments against compulsion were compelling: it would require legislation, it would have to be policed, it would alienate opinion and, in practice, it would be unenforceable if large numbers of finders chose not to co-operate. The 20-year-old voluntary scheme in Norfolk had been spectacularly successful. Similar schemes in other counties were working well. The Portable Antiquities Scheme (PAS) was duly launched in 1997.

The Portable Antiquities Scheme

The Portable Antiquities Scheme started with a pilot programme and funding for five new regional finds liaison officers. It was expanded in 1999 with a second tranche of funding for six more FLOs. Finally, in April 2002, the PAS got the funding to become fully operational with 39 FLOs giving coverage across the whole of England and Wales. The new finds liaison officers tend to be open-minded and approachable young professionals, committed to the communities they serve and proactive about getting finds recorded. They visit clubs regularly, they welcome detectorists into the museums, and they organize 'finds days', public lectures and activities for children. As a result, the recording of finds is shooting up: 13,729 in 1997–8; 20,698 in 1998–9; 31,783 in 1999–2000; and 37,518 in

2000–01. There is mass popular participation, artefacts are being salvaged, the archaeological database is expanding and our ability to understand the past is growing. It is British archaeology at its best, rooted in local communities, with opportunities for all to participate. This book and the TV series *Hidden Treasure* are testimony to that tradition.

Below: Simon Dove, metals conservator at the British Museum, working on an iron-rimmed chariot wheel fragment excavated in 2000 at Wetwang in Yorkshire.

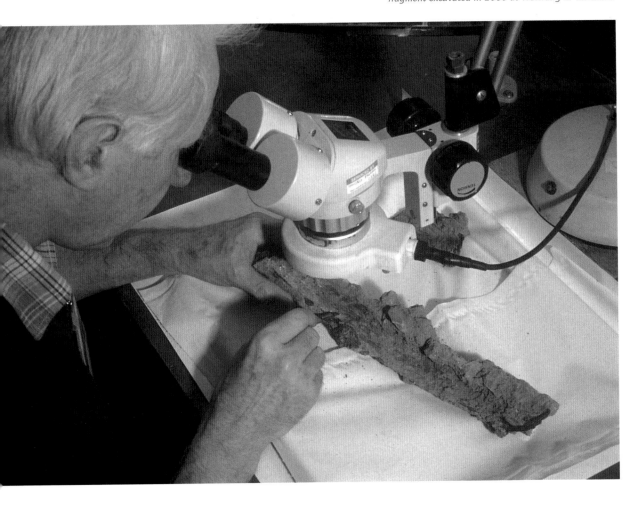

Central Unit
Roger Bland, Head of Portable Antiquities, and
Michael Lewis, Deputy Head of Portable Antiquities
and Claire Costin, Administrator
c/o Department of Coins and Medals,
The British Museum, London, WC1B 3DG
Telephone: 020 7323 8611 and
facsimile: 020 7323 8171
E-mail: info@finds.org.uk

Bedfordshire & Hertfordshire
Finds Liaison Officer
Verulamium Museum, St Michaels, St Albans,
Hertfordshire, AL3 4SW
Telephone: 01727 751 810 and
facsimile: 01727 859 919

Berkshire & Oxfordshire
Finds Liaison Officer
West Berkshire Heritage Service, The Wharf, Newbury,
Berkshire, RG14 5AS
Telephone: 01635 305 11 and facsimile: 01635 385 35

Buckinghamshire
Rosalind Tyrell, Finds Liaison Officer
County Museum Technical Centre, Tring Road, Halton,
Buckinghamshire, HP22 5PJ
Telephone: 01296 624 519
E-mail: rtyrell@buckscc.gov.uk

Cambridgeshire
Finds Liaison Officer
Archaeology Section, Cambridgeshire County Council,
Castle Court, Shire Hall, Cambridge, CB3 0AP
Telephone: 01223 717 312 and
facsimile: 01223 362 425

Cheshire, Great Manchester & Merseyside
Nick Herepath, Finds Liaison Officer
Liverpool Museum, William Brown Street,
Liverpool, L3 8EN
Telephone: 0151 478 4259 and
facsimile: 0151 478 4066
E-mail: nick.herepath@liverpoolmuseums.org.uk

Cornwall
Finds Liaison Officer
Royal Cornwall Museum, River Street, Truro,
Cornwall, TR1 2SJ
Telephone: 01872 272 205 and
facsimile: 01872 240 514

Derbyshire & Nottinghamshire
Finds Liaison Officer
Nottinghamshire County Council, Environment
Department, Trent Bridge House, Fox Road, West
Bridgford, Nottingham, NG2 6BJ
Telephone: 0115 977 2116 and
facsimile: 0115 977 2418

Devon
Finds Liaison Officer
Royal Albert Memorial Museum, Queen Street,
Exeter, Devon, EX4 3RX
Telephone: 01392 665 858 and
facsimile: 01392 421 252

Essex
Finds Liaison Officer
Museum Resource Centre, Colchester Museums
Service, Union House, 14 Ryegate Road,
Colchester, CO1 1YG
Telephone: 01206 282 931/2 and
facsimile: 01206 282 925

Gloucestershire & Avon
Finds Liaison Officer
Bristol City Museum, Queens Road, Bristol, BS1 5AQ
Telephone: 0117 922 3571 and
facsimile: 0117 922 2047

Hampshire
Jodi McCrohan, Finds Liaison Officer
Winchester Museums Service, Hyde Historic
Resources Centre, 75 Hyde Street, Winchester,
Hampshire, SO23 7DW
Telephone: 01962 848 269
E-mail: jmccrochan@winchester.gov.uk

Herefordshire & Shropshire
Finds Liaison Officer
Hereford Museum & Art Gallery, Broad Street,
Hereford, HR4 9AU
Telephone: 01432 260 692 and
facsimile: 01432 342 492

Isle of Wight
Finds Liaison Officer
Isle of Wight Archaeological Centre, 61 Clatterford
Road, Carisbrooke, Newport, Isle of Wight, PO30 1NZ
Telephone and facsimile: 01983 823 810

Kent
Andrew Richardson, Finds Liaison Officer
Heritage Conservation, Kent County Council,
Invicta House, Maidstone, ME14 1XX
Telephone: 01622 221 544 and
facsimile: 01622 221 636
E-mail: andrew.richardson@kent.gov.uk

Lancashire & Cumbria
Finds Liaison Officer
Museum of Lancashire, Stanley Street, Preston,
Lancashire, PR1 4YP
Telephone: 01772 264 061 and
facsimile: 01772 534 079

Leicestershire & Rutland
Finds Liaison Officer
Leicestershire County Council Museums Service,
Suite 4, Bridge Park Plaza, Bridge Park Road,
Leicester, LE3 4BL
Telephone: 0116 264 5810

Lincolnshire
Adam Daubney, Finds Liaison Officer
Lincolnshire County Council, Archaeology Section,
Highways & Planning Directorate, 4th Floor,
County Hall, Lincoln, LN1 1DN
Telephone: 01522 553 072 and
facsimile: 01522 553 149
E-mail: daubneya@lincolnshire.gov.uk

London
Finds Liaison Officer
Department of Early London History, Museum
of London, London Wall, London, EC2Y 5HN
Telephone: 0870 444 3852 and
facsimile: 0870 444 3853

Norfolk (Dereham)
Katie Hinds, Finds Liaison Officer
Norfolk Museums and Archaeology Service,
Archaeology and Environment, Union House,
Gressenhall, Dereham, Norfolk, NR20 4DR
Telephone: 01362 869 289 and
facsimile: 01362 860 951
E-mail: catherine.hinds.mus@norfolk.gov.uk

Norfolk (Norwich)
Adrian Marsden, Finds Liaison Officer
Norfolk Museums and Archaeology Service, Shirehall,
Market Avenue, Norwich, Norfolk, NR1 3JQ
Telephone: 01603 493 647 and
facsimile: 01603 765 651
E-mail: adrian.marsden.mus@norfolk.gov.uk

North & East Yorkshire
Simon Holmes, Finds Liaison Officer
The Yorkshire Museum, Museum Gardens, York,
YO1 7FR
Telephone: 01904 551 806 and
facsimile: 01904 651 221
E-mail: simon.holmes@ymt.org.uk

North East
Finds Liaison Officer
Museum of Antiquities, University of Newcastle,
Newcastle-upon-Tyne, NE1 7RU
Telephone: 0191 222 7849 and
facsimile: 0191 222 8561

Northamptonshire
Finds Liaison Officer
Northamptonshire Heritage, PO Box 163,
County Hall, Northampton, NN1 1AX
Telephone: 01604 237 249 and
facsimile: 01604 236 696

Northern Lincolnshire
Kurt Adams, Finds Liaison Officer
North Lincolnshire Museum, Oswald Road,
Scunthorpe, Lincolnshire, DN15 7BD
Telephone: 01724 843 533 and
facsimile: 01724 270 474
E-mail: kurt.adams@northlincs.gov.uk

Somerset & Dorset
Ciorstaidh Hayward Trevarthen and Elaine
Howard-Jones, Finds Liaison Officers
Somerset County Museums Service, Taunton Castle,
Taunton, Somerset, TA1 4AA and
Historic Environment Team, Environmental Service
Directorate, County Hall, Colliton Park,
Dorchester, DT1 1XJ
Telephone: 01823 320 200/01305 224 921 and
facsimile: 01823 320 229/01305 224 835
E-mail: chtrevarthen@somerset.gov.uk and
ehoward-jones@somerset.gov.uk

South & West Yorkshire
Finds Liaison Officer
WYAS Advisory Service, Registry of Deeds,
Newstead Road, Wakefield, WF1 2DE
Telephone: 01924 306 797 and
facsimile: 01924 306 810

Staffordshire & West Midlands
Jane Stewart, Finds Liaison Officer
Birmingham City Museum & Art Gallery,
Chamberlain Square, Birmingham, B3 3DH
Telephone: 0121 303 4636 and
facsimile: 0121 303 1294
E-mail: jstewart@wm-museums.co.uk

Suffolk
Helen Geake and Faye Minter, Finds Liaison Officers
Archaeological Section, Shire Hall, Bury St Edmunds,
Suffolk, IP33 2AR
Telephone: 01284 352 449 and
facsimile: 01284 352 443
E-mail: helen.geake@et.suffolkcc.gov.uk and
faye.minter@et.suffolkcc.gov.uk

Surrey
David Williams, Finds Liaison Officer
Surrey County Council Planning Department,
County Hall, Kingston-upon-Thames, KT1 2DT
Telephone: 020 8541 9402 and
facsimile: 020 8541 9447
E-mail: daidwilliams@surreycc.gov.uk

Sussex
Finds Liaison Officer
Sussex Archaeological Society, Bull House,
92 High Street, Lewes, East Sussex, BN7 1XH
Telephone: 01273 486 260 and
facsimile: 01273 486 990

Wales
Mark Lodwick, Finds Co-Ordinator
Dept for Archaeology & Numismatics, National
Museums & Galleries of Wales, Cathays Park,
Cardiff, CF10 3NP
Telephone: 02920 573 226 and
facsimile: 02920 667 320
E-mail: mark.lodwick@nmgw.ac.uk

Warwickshire & Worcestershire
Angie Bolton, Finds Liaison Officer
Warwickshire Museum, Market Place,
Warwick, CV34 4SA
Telephone: 01926 412 500 and
facsimile: 01926 419 840

Wiltshire
Finds Liaison Officer
Wiltshire Heritage Museum, 41 Long Street,
Devizes, Wiltshire, SN10 1NS
Telephone: 01380 727 369 and
facsimile: 01380 722 150

Magazines

There are two monthly hobby magazines for metal-detectorists. They are full of articles about great discoveries, finds identification and what is going on in the metal-detecting world. There are also plenty of manufacturers' advertisements for metal-detectors and other equipment. *The Searcher* can be obtained on subscription from The Searcher Subscription Department, Warners, West Street, Bourne, Lincolnshire, PE10 9PH, 01778 391 180, subscriptions@warners group.co.uk. *Treasure Hunting* is available from Greenlight Publishing, The Publishing House, 119 Newland Street, Witham, Essex, CM8 1WF, 01376 521 900, info@treasure hunting.co.uk, www.treasure hunting.co.uk.

The principal popular magazine for general archaeology is *Current Archaeology*. This comes out six times a year and carries articles about recent excavations and discoveries, updates on what is happening in the archaeological world, and reviews of new books. *Current Archaeology* also publishes *The Archaeology Handbook* once a year, the fullest listing of archaeological units, societies and digs available, and the best way to find out about volunteer opportunities. The magazine is available on subscription from 9 Nassington Road, London, NW3 2TX, 020 7435 7517, subs@archaeology.co.uk, www.archaeology.co.uk.

Books: general

Kevin Greene's *Archaeology: An Introduction* (Routledge) is a thorough summary of the whole range of current archaeological techniques. Good books concentrating on fieldwork techniques are Philip Barker's *Techniques of Archaeological Excavation* (Batsford) and Peter Drewett's *Field Archaeology: An Introduction* (UCL Press). To put things in context, Oliver Rackham's *The Illustrated History of the Countryside* (Seven Dials) cannot be recommended highly enough, William Hoskins' *The Making of the English Landscape* (Hodder & Stoughton) is a wonderful old classic, and Tom Williamson's *The Origins of Norfolk* (Manchester) is a brilliant case-study. *Guide to Conservation for Metal Detectorists* by Richard Hobbs, Celia Honeycombe and Sarah Watkins (Tempus) is an excellent short handbook on recovering, conserving and curating metal finds. More detailed information for excavators is provided by David Watkinson's *First Aid for Finds* (Rescue). Richard Hobbs's *Treasure: Finding Our Past* is a new British Museum publication to accompany a major exhibition opening in November 2003 as part of the museum's 250th anniversary celebrations. The political issues between metal-detectorists and archaeologists are discussed in *Metal Detecting and Archaeology in England* by Colin Dobinson and Simon Denison (Council for British Archaeology).

Books: time periods

Sadly, much archaeological writing is unbearably dull, and many archaeologists seem to make no effort to write attractively for general readers. Some periods are better covered than others. The Romanists do best (everything is relative), followed by the prehistorians, while the Anglo-Saxonists are positively dreadful. This is, therefore, a very select bibliography – coupled with a plea to some of my colleagues to try harder! *Hengeworld* by Mike Pitts (Century) and *Seahenge* by Francis Pryor (HarperCollins) are highly readable introductions to Bronze Age ritual sites by two leading experts. Tim Darvill's *Prehistoric Britain* (Routledge) is heavyweight but a sound survey of the evidence. Barry Cunliffe's

The Ancient Celts (Oxford University Press) is a colourful and wide-ranging discussion of the Iron Age, and Stuart Piggott's *The Druids* (Thames & Hudson) is a lively survey of the evidence. Julius Caesar's *The Gallic War* (Penguin Classics) can also be recommended for its dramatic account of the Romans and Celts at war. Roman Britain is exceptionally well covered. For good general surveys, there are Peter Salway's books for Oxford University Press: *A History of Roman Britain* and *The Oxford Illustrated History of Roman Britain*. Guy de la Bédoyère has produced a fine series of accessible books on different aspects of the subject. Among those currently in print in the Tempus range are *Eagles Over Britannia* (on the Roman army), *Roman Towns in Britain* and *Gods with Thunderbolts* (on Romano-British religion). Naturally, I quite like my own *The Decline and Fall of Roman Britain* (Tempus) and, for an opposite view, Martin Henig's *The Heirs of King Verica* (Tempus) is good fun. On the Anglo-Saxons, James Campbell's edited volume *The Anglo-Saxons* (Penguin) can be strongly recommended, while Martin Carver's *Sutton Hoo: Burial Ground of Kings?* (British Museum Press) is a splendid account of the site, the excavations and what it all means. Seamus Heaney's new translation of *Beowulf* (Faber and Faber) admirably conveys the atmosphere of early Anglo-Saxon kingship.

Books: finds

The Shire Archaeology series is an outstanding set of short handbooks on different categories of archaeological sites and artefacts. Among the titles of particular value to metal-detectorists and fieldwalkers are: *Anglo-Saxon Pottery*, *Celtic Coinage in Britain*, *Flint Implements of the Old Stone Age*, *Later Prehistoric Pottery in England and Wales*, *Later Stone Implements*, *Medieval Pottery*, *Neolithic and Early Bronze Age Pottery*, *Post-Medieval Pottery 1650–1800*, *Pottery in Roman Britain*, *Roman Coinage in Britain*, *Romano-British Coin Hoards* and *Samian Ware*. Greenlight Publishing has a long list of identification manuals aimed mainly at metal-detectorists, including *Pottery in Britain*, *Celtic & Roman Artefacts*, *Saxon & Viking Artefacts* and *Medieval Artefacts*. Other books deal less with basic identification than with the methodological problems involved in interpreting what finds tell us about the past. Richard Reece's *The Coinage of Roman Britain* (Tempus) can be recommended.

The Portable Antiquities Scheme

The PAS currently produces three major publications each year: the *Treasure Annual Report*, the *Portable Antiquities Annual Report* and the *Finding Our Past* newsletter (Department for Culture, Media and Sport). It also runs a popular and fast-expanding website which catalogues tens of thousands of finds (www.finds.org.uk). The PAS Central Unit can be contacted at Portable Antiquities Office, c/o Department of Coins & Medals, British Museum, London, WC1B 3DG, 020 7323 8611. There are also now finds liaison officers in all parts of England and Wales (see pages 183–5).

ACKNOWLEDGEMENTS

This book is not the result of my own research. Everything I have written is based on information supplied by numerous finders, field archaeologists, museum specialists and television producers, directors and researchers. Though I am an archaeologist myself, and though I have peered into some of the trenches and handled some of the objects featured in the TV series, I could not have written anything useful had I worked alone. This is, in the very best sense, 'the book of the series' – a book which synthesizes contributions from the many highly skilled people involved, one way or another, in the BBC's *Hidden Treasure* programmes. I am merely the mechanic who has welded the parts together.

The people who helped especially are often those whose names appear in the text. But I shall name them again here, along with others whose help was equally essential. On the TV side, there were Ian Potts, the series producer, and Clare Duncan, Monica Kupper, Kate Murray and William Spiers, the researchers for the programmes. Advising me on metal-detectors, treasure law, the Portable Antiquities Scheme and other related matters were Trevor Austin (National Council for Metal Detecting), Roger Bland and Michael Lewis (Portable Antiquities Scheme), Kevin Leahy (North Lincolnshire Museum) and Andrew Rogerson (Norfolk Landscape Archaeology). Roger, Michael and Kevin also gave valuable advice on my accounts of discoveries and their interpretation, as did all of the following: Cliff Bradshaw, Dave Cummings, Chris Fenn, Alan Meek, Dave Phillips, and Ken and Hazel Wallace (the treasure finders); Gil Burleigh, Patrick Clay, Linzi Everett, David Hillelson, John Manley, John Newman, Keith Parfitt, Vicki Priest, Simon West and Sally Worrell (the local archaeologists); and Martin Henig, J.D. Hill, Richard Hobbs, Ralph Jackson, Stuart Needham and Jonathan Williams (the specialists).

Many of these people gave a great deal of time to reading and correcting large amounts of text. For this they received no reward, and to them I am therefore very grateful. Some, seeing the finished result, may be disappointed that I did not pay better attention to their advice. I discovered, however, that perceptions of events and interpretations of finds sometimes varied among those closely involved. On other occasions, material had to be cut for lack of space, including some of the caveats and qualifications with which we archaeologists generally litter our official reports. And sometimes, I must confess, I stubbornly rejected an interpretation I disagreed with even when it was offered by someone much better qualified to judge. Needless to say, I take full responsibility for all that appears here.

Finally, my thanks go to an excellent publishing team at BBC Worldwide, whose thorough professionalism has transformed a clumsy draft into an attractive book. I am especially grateful to Warren Albers, Bobby Birchall, Linda Blakemore, Charlotte Lochhead and Sally Potter. It has been a pleasure to work with them.

Neil Faulkner, June 2003

Alan Meek 103 (both), 105, 106 (below), 109; Bridgeman Art Library 59 (copy of Greek original of 230–220 BC by Epigonos), 76 (Private Collection, engraved by Robert Havell in 1815); The British Library 138 (caption translation by Dr Tamara Romanyk); The British Museum 12 (below), 13 (below), 33, 36 (artist K. Hughes), 43 (below), 51 (both), 52, 53, 54 (both), 57, 58 (artist K. Hughes), 60, 62, 80, 120 (all), 128 (above), 142, 144-5, 154, 166, 170-1 (all), 182; Cliff Hoppitt 116-7; Corbis 14-5 (© Yann Arthus-Bartram), 30 (© Robert Estall), 150 (© Macduff Everton); Chris Fenn 16, 18, 21, 23; Dover Museum 44; English Heritage 12 (above), 28-9 (© Skyscan), 41 (© David Garner), 43 (above), 67 (© Skyscan), 74 (© Corbridge Roman Site), 128 (below), 137 (artist Peter Dunn); Gil Burleigh 108; H. Lilienthal, courtesy of Rheinisches Landesmuseum, Bonn 72; Hayley Vermeulen 98, 106, 119, 135; Helen Partridge 63; Kelvin Wilson 133; The Kobal Collection/Walt Disney Productions 156; Jason Hawkes Library 48; Jim Ashcroft 126; Michael Holford 111, 118, 134; Miranda Krestovnikoff 143; Norfolk Museums & Archaeology Service 177 (photo Dave Wicks); Robert Harding 26-7 (© Adam Woolfitt), 38 (© Schuster); Roman Baths, Bath and North East Somerset 114; St Albans Museums 13 (above), 84, 86, 87, 88, 92 (artist Alan Sorrell), 95 (both), 97, 100 (artist Peter Froste); St Edmundsbury County Council/West Stow Anglo-Saxon Village 123, 124; Skyscan 46-7 (© Farmar), 82-3, 148-9, 158-9, 160; Susan Austin 164; Sutton Hoo Research Trust (photo Nigel Macbeth) 130; Will Spiers 31, 35, 49.